In Shun Mie's Room

In Shun Mie's Room

Shun Mie Shee

iUniverse, Inc.
New York Lincoln Shanghai

In Shun Mie's Room

iUniverse books may be ordered through booksellers or by contacting:

iUniverse
2021 Pine Lake Road, Suite 100
Lincoln, NE 68512
www.iuniverse.com
1-800-Authors (1-800-288-4677)

ISBN-13: 978-0-595-36596-8 (pbk)
ISBN-13: 978-0-595-81025-3 (ebk)
ISBN-10: 0-595-36596-5 (pbk)
ISBN-10: 0-595-81025-X (ebk)

Printed in the United States of America

Contents

FOREWORD. vii

CHAPTER I SHUN MIE'S STORY 1

CHAPTER II Marriage to my Husband 46

CHAPTER III RELATIONSHIPS WITH MEN 65

CHAPTER IV LOVE AND MARRIAGE 109

CHAPTER V FINANCES DURING MARRIAGE. 128

CHAPTER VI ENDING A RELATIONSHIP 133

CHAPTER VII HEALTH 148

CHAPTER VIII RELATIONSHIPS WITH CHILDREN 158

CHAPTER IX SUCCESS STRATEGIES REGARDING
    EMPLOYMENT. 183

CHAPTER X OPENING YOUR OWN BUSINESS 188

EPILOGUE 193

FOREWORD

Having lived in this country for over thirty years, I want to share with the reader some of my thoughts about the cultural differences between life in my native country of Taiwan and life in the United States.

If one understands the Taiwanese culture and some of the adversities inherent within it, one can understand any culture where women have to learn certain coping skills in a life for which they are often ill equipped.

I will also tell how my life evolved after I came to the United States. I decided to write this book to serve as an aid and guide for women of all ages and to share the benefits of some knowledge from my personal life as well as that of some people who have been kind enough to tell me of their own experiences.

Through trials and tribulations I have come to many realizations in my life, some painful, others enlightening. Whatever struggles life brings our way, it is from these that we learn and from these that we proceed to a higher level of consciousness.

I've come to realize that self-reliance is the key to real happiness and enjoyment in life.

It is with this key concept in mind that I decided to write this book to help instill strength and wisdom within other women and to guide them through their problems and challenges in life. I want to let them know that they are not alone. It is my goal to empower women to push forward and to persist toward the achievement of their goals, even if obstacles get in the way and regardless of how difficult things might seem to be at the time. I wish to share this with you, the reader, so that you can better understand some of the adversities I faced and learn to avoid them yourself.

As an esthetician, over the years, I met hundreds of single and married women, men and teenagers. I have listened to their stories and have shared their joy and their pain. Especially when I worked with teenagers, they listened very carefully to me because my background was very different than theirs. I tell them that in this country it is easy for them to go to school and to choose what they want to be. In Taipei, in order to go to college, you had to be very rich. Yet, a lot of children don't appreciate what we have here. It is too convenient for them.

Later on they say to themselves, I wish I had done this or that. I always tell them that they are very lucky. We have no war in this country and we are free.

When people are young, they never think about their future. They don't realize that the days go by very quickly. I tell them that when they go to school, they have to learn what they want to do. Many teenagers wind up having to go back to school and re-training themselves to do what they really want to do. When you grow up, you should learn many different things so you have something to fall back on.

These teenagers listen, though. They tend to be strong willed, and they will listen to a complete stranger more than they will to their parents. I really enjoy talking with them. It's great. I have taken care of many teenagers in my field. They are the most fun to work with.

Because of these experiences with youth and with young women in particular, I realized how few women really understand how to use life's lessons to achieve a higher level of consciousness. It is for this reason that I decided to write this book of stories that these women have told me as well as the lessons I have learned from them. I hope these stories help other women gain the strength and wisdom needed to overcome any problem or challenges they face in life. I hope that they do become empowered and persist in achieving their goals no matter how difficult things might seem.

Life is ups and downs. That's what life is all about. We have happy times and sad times, and we continue to learn new things. Always learn good things, though. Don't learn the bad things in life.

When you are sad, and you think something is wrong, nothing is necessarily wrong with you. If you are healthy and working, that is a lot. If a little thing goes wrong, sometimes it feels like a big deal; but it is not. You can't get upset if there is a little something wrong because then if something really bad happens to you, you won't know how to handle yourself.

When you are upset, everything goes wrong. When this happens, your mind has to be very strong. When you think everything is wrong, and you get upset, then everything does go wrong. Try not to get upset. Sometimes it is very easy to make one little mistake that gets compounded by other things. Sometimes you can't help it if you have problems because, particularly if you are in a relationship, men seem to create problems for you. Also, in life, there are apt to be other problems along the way just because that's the way life is. You can't help it. You have to accept what happens. You must learn how to correct things when they go wrong.

How you conduct yourself when you have problems is very important. You must learn how to be strong and to think before you act. Don't be impulsive. Otherwise, things could get much worse for you. Try to work out the best result after making mistakes, and try to turn a negative situation into a positive one from which you can learn. This will strengthen you. After that, when something unpleasant comes your way, you will know how to handle it. That's what life is all about. Women today must be especially strong, mentally and physically.

For some time, I thought I was going to win the lottery. I had been buying and buying lottery tickets. But I didn't even get the numbers close. I would sometimes spend a couple of hundred dollars on tickets. I played the game, but felt a little silly because I realized it was unlikely that I would win.

With few exceptions, there generally aren't any shortcuts to success in life.

My ultimate goal in life is to help unwanted and disadvantaged children who lack proper nourishment, proper clothes, proper education, and loving homes. A designated portion of the profits of this book will be used to help the disadvantaged children in this world.

Sometimes in life, you have to go through tough times first. This is unfortunate, but that's exactly how life is. When you know this, you will finally see what life can bring you.

Everything can come to you. You can be happier, too.

Unfortunately, sometimes you have to go through bad times as well as good times. It's normal to go through a few tough times in life. When you go through tough times, you might say to yourself, "Why me?" You look at everyone else, and their lives seem to be going on in a normal way. Look at this as a challenge to make yourself stronger. Sometimes you might feel like you can't handle it, but you can. When bad times befall you, you must try to be calm and say to yourself, "Everything is going to be okay."

Sometimes, too, God tests you to see how you are going to handle things.

I have gone through many difficult times in my life. Every time something very bad happened to me that I could not control I told myself that this could be the end of me. With the illnesses I had, people usually don't survive. I didn't think I would recover.

When I arrived in the United States, I had a few tragedies. Then, when I got very sick, I often thought of when I was growing up. I got very sick then, too. I had no pills and no medication because we didn't have any in our country. I saw that with all the medication we are taking today, we don't get better. When I was young, all I knew is that I didn't really think it would be the end of my life. I always knew how strong I was growing up.

When I arrived in this country, I just trained myself to be strong because I had a daughter to take care of. I would have done anything to get better and to help her grow up. I know that I got sick then because my head was not settled. I was doing too many things. I wasn't relaxed. My mind was on too many things. I treated myself as if I was made of steel, but you can't do that to yourself. There are many women out there who are alone, like I was, and I know you have to really take care of yourself to be strong.

It's best not to worry. Don't keep unpleasant thoughts in your head. Don't let yourself get depressed. Watch your diet. I cut down the amount of every food I was taking. I watched my diet. I exercised.

I cut down my workload, too, so that it wasn't so hectic. I realized it didn't have to be that way. It wasn't worth it.

I know it isn't easy, especially when you are a single parent. The main thing is to keep yourself stress free. And, you have to be happy, no matter what. Sometimes you have much to do at home, but you don't want to kill yourself doing things. Don't pile up your bills or you will have to go through them one by one later. Don't be with friends who are negative and put you down. They're not really friends. You need to be around people who build you up.

When I had problems, I didn't date. The only way to correct my problems was to work at them day by day.

Everyone is full of free advice. This advice is not always good and it can even be terrible. It can make you feel worse because people say the wrong things to you and really bring you down.

Don't trust the advice of other people. Think everything through for yourself and sort it out very carefully and then you decide what to do. You must try to change things that are unpleasant.

Don't let other people run your life because if you let them, they can ruin it for you. No one knows how you feel except you, and no one else knows what you have on your mind. No one can do anything for you except yourself. You're the one to do it. You learn from your experience and you can be proud of yourself when you have accomplished your goals. When you have problems, don't cry to anyone. Don't be sad. Don't feel sorry for yourself. Take those things that are inside of you that are unpleasant and throw them away. Put something new there.

Ask yourself, "What is happiness?"

Happiness is when you are doing something yourself and you are doing better. Then you know that is exactly right.

You have your health. You live in a nice environment. You are not living in a war zone, like Iraq. So think about that. You have food to eat. You are not starving. You are not without clothes or a place to sleep. You are driving a car and you have everything you need. Your children are fine. They choose to be what they want.

In other countries, the children can't choose. In other countries, they have no money in their pockets and no job. Think about it. This is the land of opportunity. We have rugs on the floors in our home. We have water right here. In other countries, they have to bring water for miles and miles. Sometimes they don't eat three meals a day. They might not even have one or two. In a lot of other countries, they don't have a car to drive. They have to walk everywhere they go. We are very fortunate where we live, with our environment.

We are free.

You can make a lot of mistakes when you are depressed and upset. This can create a whole new set of problems for you and things can get worse and worse and worse. You have to put something nice into your mind. Put these nice thoughts there and let your mind follow. Then that is where your mind goes because you led it there. Life can be beautiful, if you know what to do.

In life, number one is communication. Everything is centered around communication. It is like electricity. You go from one circuit to another circuit.

You have to be friendly and nice, too. It does not take a lot to be nice. A little kindness goes a long, long way.

You have to know how to present yourself. If you start looking like you are not right, everybody is going to run away from you.

When you go through a tough time, you have to know how to handle yourself. Life is what you make it. Sometimes you make mistakes, but you learn from your mistakes. No one in this world is perfect and free of making mistakes, not even the President.

Know who you are and pay attention to yourself. You must put yourself first. If you want to have a good life, think further into the future. Don't think about the past. Don't have too many jobs. Take care of yourself.

Number two is to do what you want to do in life. Don't let anybody interfere with your goals. Everybody has a goal or wants to have a goal.

You have to keep yourself healthy. If you are not healthy, life becomes very difficult. If you are sick, say to yourself, "I am going to get better." You have to think positively and keep telling yourself that you believe in yourself. Don't listen to just anybody. Listen to yourself. If you think you are alone, you are not, really. Everybody has guardian angels. Remember that.

Have animals around the house because they are lucky and will bring you happiness. Animals are wonderful and they give you so much love. If you stay away from them for a long time, they are still very happy to see you. They don't get mad. They are always happy.

Animals can change your life. No human being will ever love you like your animals. I have grown up with dogs since I was little. If I am in the house, they follow me everywhere. They know me very well. If I tell them to do something, they do it. If I am not feeling well, they know. They heal me, too. They make me feel better.

If you have children at home, the dog will take care of and protect your children. Dogs save a lot of people's lives. When children fall in swimming pools, the dogs will automatically rescue them. They guard and protect you. They are good for your spirit. Dogs are very emotional.

Sometimes you might tell yourself, "I can't do that. I can't do this." But you can do it. It's not as hard as you might think. If you see that people are not normal, don't make fun of them. Treat them the same as anyone else.

I've found a new passion in my life and that's why I am writing this book. I am so excited to be writing it that you can't imagine. I've told only my closest friends what I am doing and they are very pleased and very supportive. They can't wait for the book to come out. They tell me how proud they are of me and they give me a lot of credit for writing a book, which is something I've wanted to do for a very long time.

I still enjoy being alone sometimes so I can think. That's how I come up with ideas for the book. I don't sleep sometimes because I am so excited about the book. I put a lot of time into it. I even stopped taking so many clients so that I could devote a lot of time and energy to the book. I am enjoying it and I am very happy. I can't wait to get up in the morning and finish the book. Right now I feel like a little kid. I'm so happy that I'm practically jumping up and down with excitement.

CHAPTER I
SHUN MIE'S STORY

My Life in Taiwan

My parents lived in a very small rural village called Chunyun, which was up in the mountains. I was born the fourth of five children, four girls and one boy. My brother, Hiro, was the second eldest child. My mother had all of us approximately a year apart from each other. She had her hands full raising all of us and taking care of the household chores. Because she had so much to do, my oldest sister did a lot of the child rearing. She actually was like a mother to me.

My first name in Taiwanese was Robie. In Chunyun, there was absolutely no governmental control; consequently, there were no taxes. Later on, China became occupied by the Japanese and the government changed the citizens' names to Japanese names. My Chinese name was changed from Shun Mie Robie to the Japanese name of Shun Mie Hotchco Cobuysee. After the Japanese left China, the Chinese government changed our names again. This time my name changed to a different Chinese name, that of Shun Mie Shee, which is still my name today. This name, Shun Mie, as interpreted in Chinese, means 'soothing and beautiful.'

Chunyun was a remote village with a population of approximately 11,000 people, several hundred miles from Tai Pai, the capital of Taiwan. The climate was very hot and humid. The main industries in the region were rubber, clothing, furniture, and rice production.

When I was little, Taiwan was controlled by the Japanese. They enslaved us. At some point during my childhood, Chiang Kai-Shek took control and relieved us from what I perceived as slavery. Life got better. We got to enjoy the fruits of our labor, rather than having to share them with the government. Today, Taiwan is completely independent, but I haven't been back since the day I left. Of course, there are many cultural differences between Taiwan and the United States.

When I was growing up, my older sister was much older than I and was like my mother, but it was my father and I who were most close. He would talk to me every night before I went to bed, and he would always tell me a story. Sometimes I would ask him to tell me a story that was not so sad.

He told me that no matter what, he wanted me to be strong. "No matter what you go through, you have to learn to protect yourself. Never be sad. Always be happy," he said.

Everywhere my father went, he took me with him so that I did not have to be home with my mother. Sometimes my father would go hunting and I would have to carry the dead animal home. On these long trips my feet became swollen because I had no shoes on.

I never met a man like my father. When a man does not treat me right, I start thinking about my father. It is hard for another man to measure up to my father.

I got along with my father very well. He did not have any boys, so he treated me like a boy. He took me places that a girl would not ordinarily go, such as hunting, fishing, and climbing mountains. I always fell.

Every time I got sick and he was worried that I could not handle it, he would tell me to imagine that I was someplace else and to put that into my head. When I was sick, I had no one with me. I was by myself. I would pray to God.

My brother went to war when Hiroshima was bombed. I was only about five years old at the time.

I remember hearing the airplanes going overhead and then they would sound the siren. It was very loud. This told everybody that we had to run down into the tunnels. We did not have radios in my village so the siren was the only way of warning us of the attack. We used to turn the lights off so the pilots would not see us.

The lights were special tree candles made of wood with natural oil in them. We used to have to take food and water down into the tunnels with us. Sometimes we did not stay in the tunnel long if we ran out of food. We had to keep moving around and we didn't stay in one place for very long. We were always running and hiding.

This lasted for a few months. I never saw the bombs drop. I only heard the airplanes and the bombs. Everybody was scared. Every time the airplanes flew overhead and we heard the bombs drop, I thought there was not going to be any tomorrow.

I knew early on that my life's calling was to help people. This became very clear to me on a shopping trip when I was eight years old. My mother took me shopping in the center of our village and I saw men giving other men massages. I was intrigued by this.

I asked my mother what these men were doing. She told me that these men were massaging the arms, necks and shoulders of their customers to relieve tension and to heal and relax aching muscles. After that day, whenever my mother went shopping, I tagged along to learn the massage technique. While she would go shopping, she would drop me off next to these men and I would learn how to heal by watching them massage.

One person would massage another person, who would massage the next person, who in turn would massage the next person, and so on and so on down the line in a chain. This chain method is hundreds of years old.

When we were out in the village shopping, I also saw people getting their hair cut. When I got home, I got scissors and I practiced cutting my three sisters' hair and practiced giving them massages. This is how my interest began and this is how the seeds for my own career were sown.

Unfortunately, when I told my mother that I wanted to do that when I grew up, she just laughed out loud at me. My mother, apparently, did not think I was capable of doing this.

In my small village, only men did this work because they had strong hands. Interestingly enough, in the large cities, only blind people did this because it was thought that sighted people could do something else to earn a livelihood.

I still have my mother's voice in my ears. She didn't talk to me. She only yelled. That's all she knew how to do. She had a lot of repressed anger.

I don't believe that my parents planned my birth and I don't think I was ever really wanted. She wanted to get rid of me since I was little. I had a need for attention and had such a loss of maternal attention. I think this drew me to seek out other people outside of our home. I was drawn to interacting with people because I didn't get the attention I desperately needed. In my career as an esthetician, I love working with people and talking with them about their experiences in life. From my early childhood this need for interaction with others molded and shaped me into the person I am today.

I never wanted to be home because no one was there for me. Children do pick up on these things, as I did.

My mother hated it when I started knitting with her yarn. She made special socks or wraps to go up your legs. We could only have one pair of stockings. She got so angry with me when I tried to knit. My father told her that the only way I was going to learn was by doing, but she didn't listen to him.

When I was about five or six years old, my mother told my aunt to come pick me up. She wanted her to keep me. I would stay there for a day or so and then run back home. Fortunately, it was not too far. It was about a twenty minute walk and even at that age, I knew the way home.

In this constant motion of getting juggled back and forth from my parents' house to my aunt's house, I began to develop physical symptoms from what I call this "see-saw effect." At around age seven, I began to get very sick from continuously being so upset and feeling so displaced. My unstable environment led to many physical problems: I had trouble eating and I began to have insomnia. I would wake up in the middle of the night and not know whose bed I was in. I was traumatized, but I wasn't aware of how bad it really was for me.

When I was about eight years old, I went to live with my older sister, her husband and their one son. There was no transportation to get to her house. I recall that it took about four hours to walk there from my parents' house. I stayed there for two years and watched the children for my sister, who worked in the rice patties. Then I went back home to live with my parents and took the older boy back with my parents to live. He was about three years old. He stayed with us from that point on and we raised him as our own.

We had a hill near us and then there were the flat lands. The Japanese had a temple there and they would go pray at it. When I was about eight or nine years old, the Japanese all left Taiwan. Before they left, they knocked down all of the buildings. So the people went and knocked down the Japanese temple so they could build new homes there.

They built quite a few houses there, and when people moved there, they didn't get any illnesses, they just died.

I don't know how many people died, but it was a lot. They had bleeding noses. My father said that they should never have built homes there where the temple had been. Sometimes the homes were so shaky that the people who lived there did not have peace of mind and could not sleep. They did not feel safe there. My father felt that this land was sacred and that these people's illnesses were caused by lack of the people's respect for the temple and for the spirits there. He felt that people were not supposed to live there.

I talked to my father about the temple. I told him that a lot of people built homes on the site where the temple had been. I asked him why all of these people died.

He said, "Wherever there is a temple, it becomes a sacred place of worship that should never be disturbed. No one should ever build a house there because it is bad luck. No one should live there. You have to tear down any building in which someone died. You should never go live there. Those buildings have to be torn down now and burned. If you live there, you could be putting your life in danger."

When I was nine years old, I remember having a bad case of malaria. I was very, very sick. My eyes and my skin were yellow and my tongue was coated white. I had no appetite. My hair was very thin and dull like an elderly woman's hair. I remember my father examining my eyes and my tongue.

After I got malaria, I was not allowed to have certain foods. My parents put me on a strict diet of ginger, white rice, red beans, sweet potatoes, mashed pumpkin, vegetables, and white potatoes for one year straight. I drank approximately five glasses of vegetable juice and herbal juice per day. I had to drink a lot of orange juice. I had to have boiled water.

I could not have any visitors other than my immediate family, just my father, my mother, my sisters. When I got sick, my family was always by my side. Every time I picked up my bag to go to school, my father would say that I was not allowed to go and I had to stay at home in bed. When I had an attack, I had chills badly and I shook like a leaf. I could barely move and I felt like ice, so they had to put at least five blankets on me.

This disease put me in great danger of swallowing my tongue because it caused febrile seizures. To prevent this, my mother would put a depressor stick in my mouth and hold my tongue down.

This illness reinforced my desire to heal others. During the illness, I was never afraid because I knew I would be okay. I felt that I had the ability to heal myself by thinking positive thoughts. It worked for me then and I started feeling like I could use that same technique to help others, but I didn't really understand how. That would not become clear to me for another few years.

When I was sick, I also learned about the healing powers of herbs and natural vegetable and fruit juices. In Taiwan, we didn't have synthetic drugs. We cured all our ailments with herbs and juices and by having a good diet. I learned a lot about the power of different herbs and I continue to use them today.

It was after this illness that I became very involved in the local Christian church. I loved to help with the children there. I remember getting all the children together and teaching them how to sing songs, dance, take care of their appearance, and present themselves on stage.

I would go help them about twice a week. Often I would go buy fabric to make the children outfits to wear for church plays. They would happily perform by dancing and singing on stage. Members of the church congregation would come to watch them. It was wonderful for the children and also for the adults who enjoyed the performances.

Many ailing people would come to the church seeking help. I would lay my hands on them and heal them and provide them with solace and comfort. I would stay with them, pray with them, and talk with them. Sometimes people asked me to go to their homes when they needed me for healing, and I would go and lay my hands on them and heal them. Sometimes I would go with a few of my girlfriends. Other times I would go by myself.

I realized that I had a special touch that helped heal many of them.

I also volunteered to travel on foot with the missionaries from the church and go from village to village to help the needy. We walked hundreds of miles. It often took two to four days to get to some of the remote villages because the pathways were so narrow and treacherous. I can still feel my feet swelling from the strain. The only way we would get to where we were going was by focusing and visualizing that we had already reached our destination. Perseverance and positive attitude kept us going. We couldn't afford to let doubt and fear enter our minds.

Some people were against the church. We would often have to hide what we did from the villagers. We would have clandestine meetings in cellars and even in caves. We had such resolve. We did not let this scare us into submission. Although these trips were scary, I know that my time with the missionaries really helped me overcome a lot of fears later in life. Knowing that I had endured great danger on those narrow footpaths and in the hostile villages gave me strength and courage to take risks and to overcome a lot of my fears.

A lot of people thought that God didn't exist. If things did not go people's way, they thought that their prayers were not being answered. If you pray for something, sometimes you don't get an answer to your prayers right away. Sooner or later, you will get an answer to your prayers, but not necessarily right away.

It is like earning money. If you earn your own money, you will respect it and not waste it. It is a different feeling if you earn the money yourself than if someone hands it to you just for the mere asking. You come to respect the value of prayer, like the value of money, when you work hard to receive it.

The most poignant memory I have of one of the missionary trips is one particular village where a teenage girl was locked up in a cage completely nude. The people in the village had locked her up because she was mentally unstable. According to the townspeople, the girl had hurt and even killed some small children.

I was mesmerized by this disheveled, dirty girl. While the other missionaries were having lunch, I sneaked away and went back to her cage alone. I started asking her questions. She refused to talk, so I asked her to blink her eyes in response to the questions I asked her. I told her my name and that I was from a far away village. I asked her if she wanted me to sing and dance for her. She responded with a blink. So I sang and danced for her. I told her that I would pray for her and that she would get better and would get out of the cage soon. I told her that she would become like me. I told her that someday she would sing and dance, and people would come to watch her perform.

Six months later, we went back to the same village. A beautiful young girl with long black hair came up to me and asked, "Do you remember me?" It was the girl who had been locked up in the cage.

She was free and she was happy. She seemed rather shy, possibly because of what had happened to her, and she did not talk much. I felt special toward her because I had an interest in helping her, and she seemed to reciprocate that feeling. We hugged and cried together. She told me that she had remembered every word that I had told her and that she would repeat those words over and over everyday until she started to see herself as free. In her vision, she was singing and dancing. I believe that it was the power of her belief that ultimately set her free.

In the Taiwanese culture, we relied on the advantages of nature. For example, in our village, we did not use synthetic make-up. We had a lot of cherry trees and we picked cherries when they were in season and cut them open to use as natural make-up. They would make our rouge and lipstick.

I never heard of anyone in our community getting addicted to drugs or alcohol. We only drank on special occasions and then we had saki, which is homemade from the rice that we grew in the paddies.

The people there were basically very happy. We raised tobacco, but we were not a society of smokers. We would dry the tobacco and hang it up in the house. Often it would rot in the fields because the people really had no demand for it. Our people had very simple lives and no stress to speak of.

We didn't have any psychiatrists or people overdosing on drugs. I never heard of those things until I came to the United States. Everybody lived the same way in Taiwan. We didn't have a huge disparity between the rich and poor the way we do here.

Everybody was friendly.

We would make our clothing from scratch. We planted thread plants that bore us thread. It would take the plants about six months to grow. We would peel the plant and then take the thread from inside the plant and roll in up in a ball. We would dye it different colors from the mud in the ground. Every time my mother was making some piece of clothing, I would take it apart. She got so mad at me.

Another natural product was a plant with a ball and seeds inside. We drained the water and threw the seeds out. Inside of the ball was a small ball, like a cherry, which had soap in it. We used it on our clothes and in our hair. It made our hair so shiny that it glistened just from the washing.

The clothes we had would last forever. My mother would make everything very large because she wanted us to grow into the clothes. We had only two outfits of clothing each. I would call my sister's clothing a "laundry bag."

My sister would call me a "monkey" because I was so skinny. My mother told me that I could not go outside because the birds were going to eat me. It took a long time before I would go near the birds because I thought that they really were going to eat me up. My sisters tortured me so much that I could not wait to get out of the house. They were mean.

When I was growing up, I was surrounded by different kinds of dogs, some big and some small. The small dogs were temperamental. I trained my dogs and taught them how to behave. When I gave them a command, they did what I said. They would all look at me and wag their tails. When I was sad, they could tell. They give me a funny look. When I went for a walk, they all went with me.

One day my father, my neighbor's son, Chu, and I went for a long walk into the country. It took about four hours to get to where my father had a house there. The dogs went with me. On the way there, the dogs disappeared into the woods. As soon as we got there, they all appeared again. I told them it was getting dark, and that they better not leave. I would make a fire. If they left, I would tie them up and discipline them. They all stayed with me.

When we arrived in the country, we stayed there for four or five days. My father wanted to go there to set traps so we could get some food. We caught rabbits and deer. I tied the dogs up at the country house so the dogs would be safe and then I stayed with the dogs at the house. The dogs had to learn to walk on the trail when they were with us because the traps were set. Those dogs were very smart.

My father asked Chu to help set the traps. They hooked up long wires to hold the traps down so the animals wouldn't drag the traps away. They also dug deep holes in the ground so that the animals would fall into them. We would cut the bark off a tree as a sign that there was a hole and to warn us not to go near there.

We tied a big rope to the tree, too, so that if someone fell down into the hole, they could pull themselves out.

The day after they set the traps, my father and Chu would go collect the animals we caught and bring the food back home so we could clean and cook it on a spit, gradually turning the meat on the fire. Later we would dry the meat and then put salt on it to preserve it because we didn't have any refrigeration.

We didn't use guns to catch the animals, although my father did have a homemade gun for emergencies. We sometimes hunted with bows and arrows, though. My father taught me how to shoot very well. We would shoot arrows into the holes in trees, too, so we could practice our skills. My father made sharp points for the arrows, but they were hard to make. My father would have to get the steel very hot over the fire and mold it into the shape of an arrow. I would carry the bag for the arrows.

We had knives to throw, too. For practice we would throw the knives toward a hole in the tree to learn how to defend ourselves in the event of an emergency.

One day when I was about sixteen years old, I went for a walk in the desert with all of my dogs but one, the one who walked slowly. She stayed home. We were looking for wild mushrooms. We found them, picked them, dried them out in the sun, and later sold them in my village. Those mushrooms would last for years.

On this day, all of my dogs got lost. I got lost, too, for about an hour. I screamed and called my dogs. I cried. I kept calling my dogs, but they wouldn't answer. I got even more lost. I panicked.

Later on, the dogs started to howl. They were looking for me, too. Their eyes were so sad. They finally found me. We still did not know how to get home. So I followed them while they led the way, and we finally arrived home, much, much later.

Dogs are very good to have. Even though you are alone, you don't feel so alone. They don't yell at you or say bad things to you. If you don't feel well, they stay close to you. Sometimes, an animal can heal you if you are sick. They can be your best friends. They are very good company.

When I was sick one time, I know my dog could feel it. His eyes were red and he looked sad. My dogs didn't wag their tails anymore when I was sick because they knew that I wasn't feeling well. They were sad. They dragged me everywhere and made me go for a walk with them. I felt good with the dogs when I went far away in the country.

My mother would take corn and cook it in the corn husks. We had a lot of dried food, but we had to cook it with water and we often did not have water.

One time we did not have any rain for a long time. The crops were all dry. The water also came from a reservoir, but it had become dry. Everybody was praying and hoping for it to rain. Then it started to rain. Everybody was so happy, they sang.

My brother, Herosi, never returned from the war. That caused my parents a lot of unhappiness in their lives. They cried a lot. After that, I pretty much ran around by myself and they ignored my sisters and me. I think my father died because he had a broken heart due to my brother's death. Herosi was probably in his late twenties when he died. He always told me it was not good to worry.

My sisters would always say, "No man will marry you because you are so skinny and bony."

My mother was friends with one woman and my parents finally decided to match me up with her son. Then I saw another boy, Chu, that I liked. I told my mother I would not marry the first boy.

I ran away from home later, when I was seventeen, because I refused to marry him. I went to live in the big city with my girlfriend. I wanted to see the world. I had always said that, too.

I fell deeply in love with Chu, my neighbor's son. I still remember what he looked like. He was very thin, tall and handsome with dark hair. He didn't know anything except me. The only time I really had fun was when I was with Chu. He was devoted to me. He always wanted to feed me and take care of me. I had told him how my mother treated me.

He would tell me all the things about his family life, too. He was the youngest of four children, three boys and one girl in his family. He was very active. Every time he went hunting and fishing, he brought something home to me. He gave us half of his catch because we had four girls and one boy in our family and the girls couldn't go hunting and fishing.

That was one reason why my mother became so distraught when my father died. Boys were very important to the family and we had none. Girls were de-valued and looked upon as secondary creatures, as basically a type of impediment.

My male friend, Chu, and I knew each other for years because we grew up together. I spent a lot of my free time with him. We used to go "pan gold" together. We had to bring the dirt up from the mines.

I remember once he cooked dinner for the two of us. He made chicken, rice and vegetables. He loved to cook for the two of us. He wanted to be sure I ate well because I was so skinny.

One night Chu and I got together and we took all of the dogs for a walk in the countryside. We were rather young. Our parents never recognized that it was anything more than friendship. They thought that we were just children who were playing together. Our parents were busy with other things, and they didn't understand us and didn't recognize our relationship.

One night Chu told me, "Even though we might not be together forever, I will always be with you." The full moon was out and it was so bright that it illuminated the entire woods. It was surreal. We laughed together and we talked about a lot of things. He started talking about how people saw ghosts in that area, and for the first time, we held hands. He told me not to look behind me. I think he was trying to scare me so I would get close to him and hold his hand. Before that, I had been reluctant to hold hands with him.

As I mentioned, I had a very difficult relationship with my mother. To make matters much worse, one day when I was about sixteen years old, my mother told me to come into the kitchen and sit down at the table. She had a stern look on her face.

"Sit down," she said, "I have something to talk to you about. There is something I have to tell you."

I didn't even know what she was going to say, but I immediately developed a sick feeling in the pit of my stomach. Instinctively, I knew that she was going to talk with me about something very heavy.

She said, "Remember that day, when we were shopping for vegetables in the city and I pointed out a man to you whose name I told you was Li?"

"Yes, I think remember," I said. "I wasn't really paying very much attention to him." Li was to be my arranged husband.

When I was about 12 years old, my sister was pregnant and expecting her first child. I asked why her stomach was getting bigger and bigger, and my mother told me it was because she had a baby inside. I told my mother that it was going to be a boy.

I was very curious how the baby was going to be born. My mother told me that I could not go too far away from the house so I stayed close to watch my sister because I wanted to see how the baby would be born.

My sister walked a lot for exercise, and her feet would swell. I would massage her scalp, her feet, and her back.

We did not have any doctors, so we had to do everything ourselves. One day she told me that she had a pain in her stomach. I panicked. My mother told her to go lie on the bed and she went to get towels and sheets ready.

My sister lay down. Ten minutes later she said she was in very bad pain. I called out to my cousin and then my cousin and my sisters all came to be by her side. We all stood there, watching her. None of us knew what to do. We just watched.

The baby was a boy, as I predicted.

My cousin held the baby upside down by his feet and tapped him on his behind and he started crying. Everybody was happy.

After that, if anybody had a baby, I would go stay with her and help comfort her. I used to love see women having babies. I enjoyed it and got used to seeing the babies being born.

When I was fourteen years old, I went by myself with my dog to the country, where we had a small house. A typhoon came and destroyed the bridge, so I could not go back home. I was stuck.

Two days later my father came to give me food. He tried to throw it across the river, but the food wouldn't reach the other shore. The current was too strong and the water rose too high.

I had to cook grasshoppers over a flame. Then I ate them. I had wood and matches so I just barbecued the grasshoppers. I also ate wild vegetables that were very bitter. I had a bow and arrow, too, which I could shoot because I had gone hunting with my father previously. There were two different kinds of rabbits there. One kind jumped around; the other kind climbed trees. I shot and cooked the rabbits that climbed trees, but these rabbits had very little meat on them. I was so hungry.

After that, when I was about sixteen, I went with the missionaries to a village about three days from my village. We went on foot, as there wasn't any transportation. There was a narrow path up the side of the mountain where we had to walk to get to the village. The path was dangerously narrow, so much so that you had to walk putting one foot carefully and slowly in front of the other. If you slipped, you would fall down the cliffs of the mountain. You couldn't look down. You had to look straight ahead. When we passed that scary part, we all took a deep breath. When we got to the village, it was beautiful. Everybody was relieved and very happy.

The main agricultural activity there was farming rice, potatoes, corn, and vegetables and raising pigs and chickens. They had buffaloes that pulled the carts in the rice paddies. Everybody looked well and happy. They did not have any worries.

They had churches, though. We would go to all the churches in the different villages of that area to visit and meet the different people and worship with them. There were many villages and many people. The towns were small, but some villages had teachers.

There was a hospital that was far away from any of the villages. We went there to worship with the missionaries. When we got there, we went to different churches. If the village didn't have a church, that meant that they were against religion, so we would take those people who were interested and worship in a secret place, such as in a basement or in someone's house. We used to hide our Bibles because we were afraid of the villagers. Some of them were aggressively against religion, but others were eager to worship.

One day we went to a village where we heard a story about a man named Toya from that village. He had died and had risen from the dead.

It was our custom that we had to wait three days to bury people, but this man was never buried. He was put in the coffin but they hadn't put him in the ground yet. People went to see him after he died to pay their respects, but he was not there anymore. He had risen from the dead and afterward, he walked over to the church. He told everybody there that he had died and that he had risen from the dead. He told the children at the church to tell everybody that he had come back.

People all over the village were talking about him, and we heard that he was still in the church. Everyone was rushing over there to meet him. They were begging Toya to get up on stage and speak.

I was young then, but I remember his face. He looked like he was about thirty-five years old. The crowd was chanting his name, "Toya, Toya, Toya" and asking him to speak.

Finally, he got up on stage. He had no shoes on.

He said, "I've never been on stage in my whole life. I never read the Bible and I've never been in church before. A few days ago, I died and saw Jesus. Then I came back to life. I woke up in my coffin. When I died and met Jesus, he told me that we are all his children. He said that you don't have to go to church to pray and that you can pray anywhere you are. Jesus told me to spread his word from the Bible. God told him that he had to wake me so I could spread God's word."

Toya went on, "Jesus told me that he knew everything that I did on this earth. He said that in my lifetime there were some people whom I should have helped, but I didn't do anything. I had a farm and I let the food rot instead of giving it to people who needed food. I never made a speech before and I never sang before, but I'm here to talk to you about God and sing songs in praise of him. I never went to school and I never learned how to count, but I can tell you the exact number of days the earth has been in existence."

He knew the number. All the people reached out to touch him, and he rejuvenated people when they went near him.

This event touched everybody's heart.

Toya then began to sing songs so sensitively that it made you feel enlightened and very spiritual. A lot of people were crying just from listening to him. He told everybody that he came back to earth to teach everyone God's word. Everybody was drawn to him. His words were so interesting. He told us he would be coming back again.

Everyone came to church to listen to him. His feet were sweating profusely because he was standing in the church talking to the people for so long. I remember getting tired, too, because I listened to him for so long.

Even though Toya never had sung songs before, he somehow knew the words to the songs and when he sang, the words came out beautifully. He preached wonderfully, too, although he had never read the Bible before.

There were so many people crowding in to see Toya that it was difficult to get close to him. People came from all over to see him and to listen to him sing and preach God's word. He told people that he hadn't known if there was a god before, but now he was convinced that there was a god. He said God helped him to become the man he suddenly now was and to learn the things he learned overnight.

At one point Toya said, "God said we learn, we work hard, we cry, we are here, and we struggle. One day, when we go to his place, we don't have to do that anymore. God said there will not be any tears anymore and there will be no worries."

When I heard those words, I cried.

Eventually I had to go back to my village and when I did, I told them all about Toya. I told them that he said that when he died, the women all looked the same, and that they were all dressed in white and that the men looked healthy and looked different than we do

I told them that he had a beautiful voice, and you could hear it all over the village. He just closed his eyes and sang the songs. It was so beautiful. He was on stage and prayed for us to understand and fully accept Jesus' words. He proclaimed that there was only one son of God. He said, "We are all Jesus' children."

I told them that Toya said that Christ could see and hear us, but that we could not hear and see him.

Toya had said, "If we know him, he can be our friend as long as we live.

When you are walking somewhere, always keep other people in mind and help them. Jesus preached about kindness. He said, 'Don't hurt yourself and don't hurt others.' If your neighbor calls you to help him, then you should do what you can for him. If you can take care of yourself, then you can take care of others, too. If you walk in the street or go anywhere, you should stop and help those people who need help."

I told everyone in my village that Toya had continued, "Your eyes should always be open to other people's needs. If you help people, other people will always be there to help you. You need to respect elderly people because here they throw older people around. They don't respect them. If you are nice to people, they are nice back to you. The good things you do will always come back to you in the end."

After I told them of all of this, they all went back to their homes and we all talked about what Toya said. Everyone talked about him for a very long time.

Everywhere I went, I heard people talking about him, and they were in awe of him. Everyone was so impressed with him and his message to the community.

After that, I always felt like his words were with me. He really had a strong impact on me. To this day, I remember all of the things he said to me. When people talk about the Bible to me, I relay this story to them because I still remember it as if it were yesterday.

My mother finally said, "Well, I decided that you should marry Li, and I am making arrangements for you two to marry each other."

At that time all marriages were arranged by parents. I had only seen Li that one time in the village. My mother and his mother were very good friends and they used to do things together. Somehow, they finally decided that this marriage between Li and me should be arranged to make us all a "family of convenience."

When my mother told me this, I was so terrified that I couldn't say anything. I was so numb I was literally speechless. Even if I expressed my feelings to her, I knew that it wouldn't make any difference anyway.

It was the Chinese custom that you had to do what your parents told you to do. If they arranged a marriage for you, you didn't dare speak out against it. If you didn't do what they told you, your whole family would become embarrassed and would lose face in society. Your family would be ostracized. You had to do what they told you. You had no choice.

I was devastated by the news of this plan to arrange my marriage to Li. I knew I could never be with him because I didn't love him.

After my mother told me about the marriage, I ran outside looking for Chu. First, I went to his house, but no one was home. I was becoming even more upset now because I couldn't find him. I had to find him.

After running all over the village for two or three hours, I finally found him. By that time, I was very much out of breath. He jokingly asked me if someone was chasing me.

"Chu, this is not funny," I said. "Please don't joke with me now. I have to talk with you right away. I've been running all over creation for hours to find you. I have to talk with you right away. I have to talk with you."

Then he said, "Hotch, you are out of breath and you look pale. What's the matter? Let's walk. You can tell me what's wrong."

I said, "I hate my mother. I can't go home."

"Maybe we should go for a walk into the country," he said, "and go see my mother."

I said, "Okay."

We walked for several hours and we went to the country to Chu's parents' house. By the time we got there, it was dark.

We didn't have telephones where we lived because it was so rural. Only people who lived in the big cities, like Tai Pai, had telephones. Because we didn't have phones, our accepted custom was to just drop in on people we wanted to visit. We knew someone was home because we smelled smoke when we were far away and when we got closer, we saw smoke coming from the chimney.

Even though his parents didn't know we were coming, they were glad to see us. His mother's name was Toomi and his father's name was Tamou.

A few of my dogs followed us there. I was so exhausted by the time we got there that I was ready to collapse. I was emotionally and physically drained by all of the events of the day.

They didn't have sofas, so I lay down on one of the beds. I couldn't talk. Chu covered me up with a blanket and gave me a pillow.

He said, "Just lie there and relax. I won't let anything bad happen to you. You don't have to go home if you don't want to. I'm going to go outside and get some wood for the fire so my mother can make dinner for us. Just lie there and rest. You can go to sleep if you want to."

I was so devastated that I stayed at his mother's house with Chu for a week so I didn't have to go home. His mother was very kind to me. She and I got along very well together. When we had originally left for the mountains, I didn't have time to bring any clothes with me, so I had to wash my clothes every night. His mother was kind enough to loan me some clothes to wear while my clothes were drying by the fire. By the next day, my clothes would be dry and I would put them back on.

The first night there, I slept for two or three hours. When I awoke, I wasn't sure where I was at first. I can still remember the smell of fresh vegetables, though, which came wafting into the bedroom where I lay.

When I realized I was at Chu's mother's house, I called out to him, "Chu, Chu, where are you?"

He came running into the bedroom and sat on the side of the bed. Gently he stroked my long silky black hair away from my face. He held my hand.

"Now, my sleeping beauty awakes," he said. "I'm glad you had a nice sleep after all that. You must have been very tired. Are you hungry, Hotch?"

I felt so secure in that very moment. I actually believed that nothing bad could happen to us. The horror of the day evaporated. I felt so at peace that I didn't want to talk to him right then about what had happened because I didn't want that reality to affect us.

It felt so good just being there with him in the softness of the moment.

After we had dinner, we went outside. The sun was still up. We walked off into the mountains and had a beautiful view of the farmhouse below.

Chu brought a blanket with him and we sat on the ground facing one another. We sat there and leaned back and watched the sun sink into the earth with its broad array of colors, pink, purple, blue yellow, and red. I remember how beautiful it was.

Chu gently caressed my chin with his hand.

"You have beautiful brown eyes," he said. He pulled my long hair back into a ponytail and tied it with a piece of white cloth that he pulled out of his pocket. I recognized it as the same cloth he had tied the cucumbers with when he was working on the farm.

He reached over and stroked my hand. "Hotch, do you feel ready to talk to me yet about what's wrong?"

I looked up at him, almost ready to cry. I was very sad again. My voice was choking. I couldn't get the words to come out.

"Don't worry. I won't let anything happen to you," he said. "Did someone hurt you?"

I took a deep breath and said, "Chu, my mother told me that I have to marry Li. Do you know who he is?"

He looked perplexed. "Who is that?" he asked.

"He is the son of my mother's good friend," I said.

Chu said, "We can run away together. Don't worry. I won't let you marry someone you don't want to marry."

"I wish that you and I could always be together," I said. "I can't imagine not having you in my life anymore. If I have to marry Li, I will never be able to see you again. You know that, don't you?"

"I understand," Chu said. "You don't have to marry him. You and I will be together."

I said, "I won't marry anyone else except you."

Chu's words were comforting to me. I wanted to believe his words and his strong faith that we would be together forever.

We sat there looking at the sunset, holding hands. He put his arm around me and I relaxed my body against his chest while we talked some more. The sunset was beautiful.

When we left, it was dark. We decided to run down the hill to see who would get home first. The two dogs ran with us. Chu and I ran neck and neck. Then he let me get a little bit ahead. I know he let me because he was unquestionably faster than I was. Finally, when we got near the house, Chu spurted ahead of me and up to the house.

"Hotch, you're not going to win first prize for this one, but you are a close runner up, so just for that, you are going to get second prize, which is this…"

He went and picked a bouquet of beautiful wild flowers that were growing nearby and he handed them to me.

"For the runner up," he said.

I took the flowers in my hand and pulled them up to smell them. They were delightful.

He drew one of the flowers out of the bunch and put it behind my ear. "You look beautiful, Hotch," he said. "Your cheeks are so pink from running."

In the distance, we could hear his mother calling us.

"Chu! Hotch! Where are you? I've been looking for you," Toomi called. "Please come! It's getting dark and we must get the vegetables in."

Those tender moments between Chu and me were finally interrupted by his mother's calls.

We called back to her so she would know where we were and then we ran over to her.

She said, "It's getting dark. I know you wanted to pick some vegetables before it gets too dark."

When we got to the garden and were by ourselves again, I said to Chu, "We have to go home tomorrow because it's teenage night."

"I can't wait." Chu said.

We talked while we began picking the green beans, cucumbers, carrots, and corn. We had to dig the sweet potatoes out of the ground with the metal instruments my own father had made. After we dug the sweet potatoes out, we prepared the soil by flattening it out so the next generation of potatoes could grow.

In those days we would plant peanuts and pick them once a year. We would plant one peanut about every ten inches in the ground and each plant would yield many peanuts. When the plant was mature, the leaves, which were low to the ground, would start to dry out and fall off. That meant that it was time to pick the peanuts. Peanuts were very valuable as a food storage item because they would keep for a very long time. The same held true for rice and beans.

Chu, his mother and I worked hard gathering the vegetables, and then we had to put them into bags so we could carry them home with us the next day.

After we were finished gathering the vegetables, we went inside. The dinner Toomi fixed for us smelled very good. She made two different kinds of vegetables as well as cucumbers, sweet potatoes and rice. We didn't have any meat that night and we didn't eat much meat in general. My favorite foods were sweet potatoes, corn and rice.

We talked for a while and then Chu went outside to take care of the farm chores. He had to take care of the cold storage for the vegetables we'd picked.

I was left alone with Toomi in the house. Toomi said, "You two practically grew up together. The time has gone so fast. I have known you since you were a little girl. You two have become adults." I was seventeen then.

"We are adults," I said. "You know, Toomi, I ran away. I didn't tell my mother."

"Why didn't you?" she asked.

"She doesn't worry about me very much, "I said. "She knows I know how to take care of myself. If she really wanted to find me, she would look here for me. The same goes for my sisters. Besides, I had an argument with her."

"What did you argue about?" Toomi seemed surprised. "When we lived next door to you in town, I never heard your mother argue with you."

"She told me that I was seventeen now and getting older. She and my father decided to pick the man I was going to marry. I have a question for you. Did you and Tomou have an arranged marriage?"

"Yes. But from the moment I saw him, I liked him. He was very tall and very handsome."

"That sounds like Chu and me. It was like you had been dating Tomou, wasn't it? When my mother told me she had arranged my marriage to Li, I got very upset. That's why I came up here with Chu. I don't want to get married yet. I want to see more places and meet different people before I get married."

"How about the churches you go to?" she asked. "You get to go different places."

"That's different. I do enjoy that, though," I said.

She thought for awhile and then said, "Yes, you are right."

"I cannot marry Li," I said. "I don't even know him. I saw him once from a distance. I see his mother all the time because she comes to visit my mother. They are best of friends."

Toomi asked, "Does Chu know?"

"Yes, he knows," I said. "He is my boyfriend. We've grown up together. We understand each other and we know each other very well. I don't think we should be separated now. I want to stay away from home. I can't go back there now. I'm too upset."

"Where are you going to go?" Toomi asked.

"I don't know yet."

"This is not good," Toomi said. "Chu is very sensitive. He takes things very seriously. And when he wants something, he gets it."

"We will spend a lot of time together," I said. "We will walk the dogs together. We will be having teenagers' night tomorrow, too, so we have to go home soon."

Afterward, Chu and I departed and traveled back to Chunyun.

The next night was teenagers' night in our village. All of the young people from the different villages got together to dance and sing. Some of the teenagers danced very well, and some of their voices were very good. When we danced, we danced differently than we do here. If I had someone to sing with, I would sing, but I wouldn't sing much alone. Most of the others would dance together. I didn't have any confidence when it came to dancing.

I loved to listen to one of the girls, named Que, who was from our village. She sang extremely well and had started singing when she was very young. When she started singing in church, people would go and listen to her because she sang gospel so beautifully. She got to be so popular that she traveled to other churches and sang for them. When she traveled, some of the other girls would travel with her to keep her company.

Sometimes, when she sang those songs, we would all join in. Even me. I enjoyed that camaraderie. I miss it very much because it was so soothing. When there were holidays or special occasions, we would invite people from other villages to see us perform. We would dance to the music and celebrate. Our society was a happy one.

The ones who could not sing or dance well would sit and play the drums of many different sizes that were hand made from animal skins. We loved to entertain each other. Sometimes we would get together when a neighbor family was a little bit unhappy and we would pray for them.

We would all listen to those who sang and watch those who were dancing. We would wrap vegetables in banana leaves and cook them outside over the fire.

We all sang one song I remember, "We Will Always Be Together." Each one of us then told a story. My story was that I would like to have a lot of children. I knew that I wanted to live far away from home.

When we talked, we shared our individual ideas. In those days we didn't say bad words. I didn't even know any bad words until I moved to the city and learned the slang words.

We ate papayas, peaches, bananas, and oranges. We had water to drink. We didn't drink liquor at all. Everybody was happy. We had nothing to worry about.

The only thought nagging my mind was what my mother told me about the arranged marriage with Li. I tried not to think about it that night.

Some weeks later I got very sick. I had no appetite and I couldn't eat. I had a fever, a cold and chills. My father tried giving me all kinds of herbs. Nothing seemed to work.

I was skinny to begin with, but I grew extraordinarily thin. Everybody was worried about me. They thought I was going to die.

Chu came to visit me. I had seen his father Tomou from my window. He was peeling something that looked like it had once been alive and I watched him.

Chu had told his father how ill I was, so Tomou cut off a piece of this thing, which had been dried for a long time. Chu gave it to me. It looked like barbecued fish or maybe some type of eel, but Chu told me it was a dried fish. I ate it.

Within two to three weeks, I felt much better. My fever went down. I started to run around like a normal child again.

Much later on, Tomou told me that the fish he had given me to eat was really a snake.

I threw up. I couldn't eat for several days. My mother finally went to Tomou and told him that he made me sicker than I was before. To this day, I hate the notion of snakes.

Chu would come over to the house to visit me. Every time he came, my father would put him to work. My father taught him how to do many things. Together they made wooden bowls of all different sizes. Everything was hand made then. They made forks and spoons. They made belts from the skins of animals, and my father would sell them. My father would make buttons from the hides of animals.

Chu loved my father very much, and my father loved him as if he was his son. It was a comfort to my father having Chu around, because after losing Hiro in the war, my parents were left with four girls.

After my mother told me about the arranged marriage to Li, I was very upset. Part of me felt like I didn't want to live anymore, while the other part of me knew I had to go on.

I went to talk with my father. I wanted to have a private talk with him.

"Why don't we go up into the country where the air is fresh and we can think?" he said.

"Daddy, I want to be with you. I don't want Mom to come with us."

"That's no problem," he said. "It will just be the two of us going."

So we walked a long ways to our house in the country. We arrived there in the evening and as soon as we got there, I went to gather the wood from outside. We started a fire. My father went outside and got some food from the cold storage and he began cooking something for us to eat.

After that trip, my mother forbade me from seeing Chu anymore.

I told her, "Don't wait for me for dinner tonight. I won't be here."

I ran with my dog to see Chu in the countryside. I wanted to get there before dark. It took me two hours, and when I got there, I was out of breath. It was almost dark by that time.

Chu and his family were inside the house having dinner. He stood up, surprised to see me.

"Hotch, what are you doing here now?" he asked. "Don't you know how dangerous it is on foot at this time of day?"

"I know. I wanted to see you."

"Come, sit down and have something to eat with us," his mother said.

"No, thank you. I'm not hungry."

The family was just finishing dinner.

"Come on, let's go outside," Chu said. "Look at all my plants. They are doing very well with all the rain we are having. Everything is so lush and green."

We strolled for a while. Then he said, "Okay, now tell me what's wrong."

"I got very upset with my mother so I ran all the way here," I said. "It took me two hours to get here. I had to talk to you right away. My mother made me so mad. She told me that I can't see you anymore. But she can't stop me. We can always see each other at church. We can meet down by the lake. Christmas is around the corner, too, and we will be having a lot of rehearsals, basically every other night."

We had several groups in the choir that sang different melodies and different ranges. When we all learned our parts, we sang the song together and it was beautiful.

I said, "We can see each other there. No one is going to separate us."

"That's a good idea," he said.

"After the rehearsals, I will come to your house next door. My mother will think I am visiting your mother and your sister."

So we started sneaking around. Everything was okay for short while. After rehearsal one night, I said, "Chu, how did you like the rehearsal tonight?"

"Oh, I like my group. They all have nice voices."

"After church, if you don't see me," I said, "we will just know to meet at the lake. After that, we will go visit your brother. I know it is a little ways, but no one will be around to bother us or to spy on us."

After church, we went there and spent some time with his family. He stayed on there and I went home afterward.

Before I left, I had asked him, "When will you be home?"

"Tomorrow," he said,

"Then I will see you at the rehearsal the day after tomorrow," I said.

He walked me outside. He was holding my hand and sweetly saying good-bye. He was always sensitive and kind to me.

Two days went by and I saw him at the next church rehearsal. He said, "Did you get home okay the other night?"

I said, "Yes, I ran all the way home."

"Are you going home tonight?"

"I am going to my home in the village, but if your mother is home, I will come over," I said. "If she is not home, I can't come over because my mother will be over there banging on your door for me to come home."

My mother began watching me like a hawk. She knew I was sneaking around and meeting Chu. She watched me all the time. Sometimes she would send my sister to look for me and report back to her.

Then she and her girlfriend started talking about the wedding plans. She had begun to make me so angry that one day I finally went to her and said, "Don't you understand that I'm not going to marry Li no matter what you or anybody else says. I'm going to leave here. I'm running away. There is no way I can marry that man."

I didn't know what to do. I couldn't wait to leave there and get a real job so I could live the way I wanted to.

"Can't you see that I am in love in Chu?" I asked her. "I grew up with Chu. He's the only man I know. If I don't marry him, I will never get married. You're not going to see me anymore. I'm leaving."

"You are very young," my mother told me. "You don't know what's outside there in the world. Where do you think you are you going to go? You never have never been out of the countryside in your life. This is all you know."

"You are forcing me to leave," I said, "and now I have to go far away because I can't stand it here anymore."

I said all of these words to her, yet I was very fearful of the outside world and how I was going to survive out there. Part of me was very happy that I stood my ground with her on this issue, while the other part of me was terrified because she was actually correct. I was young and inexperienced with worldly things. I don't think she took me seriously at all because I had threatened to leave home so many times before that.

When I was seventeen, I went into the city once and split off by myself to go shopping. We had a big earthquake. The entire earth kept moving under my feet and the ground split into a huge crack right beneath my feet. Fortunately, a man came to my rescue by grabbing me and saving me from falling through the crack. It was as if a guardian angel was with me.

After that, I never wanted to go anywhere alone. I got scared to be by myself. If anything moved, I could not move. I just sat in one place. This stayed with me for a very long time. My father kept telling me to think of something else and to think forward into the future.

Meanwhile, a sad thing happened in the village. Toyoko, who was 22 years old, was very much in love with my cousin, Yang. They had been seeing each other for a long time.

I was very close to my cousin. He always helped my father with everything. He was a very strong man and was also very good looking. He was a builder and had made many homes.

One day Toyoko came to me and we went for a walk in the country. She seemed very upset and sad, and she was crying. She told me she wanted to kill herself. She asked me what the fastest and least painful way of dying was. She wanted to know whether she should poison herself or hang herself.

I asked her why she wanted to die.

She told me that her mother was going to force her to marry a man named Hia. She hardly knew him and didn't love him. She said she was madly in love with Yang.

I told her that she should go marry Yang and live in another town. She told me that she didn't want her parents to lose face. Our Taiwanese customs were very engrained. She didn't want to lose the respect of her parents and of Hia's parents. She said there was no way that she could marry Hia. She told me that the best thing for her to do was to kill herself.

The next day she hung herself in the woods.

I was very unhappy about what happened to Toyoko. I felt like I was to blame.

After that, I went to talk with my father.

"Dad, I want to talk to you. Do you realize that mom is making my life unbearable with Chu? Did you hear about what happened to my girlfriend, Toyoko? A few weeks ago, they found her clothes on the ground. She had hung herself in a big tree. She was so upset because her parents told her that she had to marry someone she didn't love."

"Oh, no. What a tragedy!" my father said.

"Toyoko and I were very close," I said. "She would come over to the house a lot so she could see Yang. She used to come to my house and take me everywhere she went. The only way she could see my cousin was to come and visit me. Then they fell in love. I feel very bad that I never told any of this to Yang. I feel like it is my fault because I never said anything."

Then I told him, "Not only that, but I had another close girlfriend whose parents arranged a marriage for her. She did not love the man either. With this other girlfriend, Uty, the same thing happened. When you are seventeen or eighteen, you have to get married. If you get married any later than that, you're considered to be an old maid."

"It's not your fault," my father said. "Don't say anything. No matter what, if you go through a hard time in life, never resort to killing yourself."

"I am going through something like Toyoko went through," I told my father. "My mother says I have to marry Li, but I am not in love with Li. I am in love with Chu. I know there is nothing you can do because that is the custom."

"This has to be changed," my father said. "This can't stay like this. A lot of young people have taken their lives because of arranged marriages. This can't be changed overnight, though. The parents think that they are protecting their children by choosing a nice family for them, but it is not what the children want. I have to speak with everybody in the village."

"I understand, Dad," I said, "But I'm going to run away. I'm not sticking around here. You may not see me for a while because I am going to live with my sister. I need to go away to think."

I told Chu I had to leave. He really didn't take me seriously, either. He had gotten used to listening to me moan and whine about my situation, so he didn't believe me because he had heard it so many times.

I did run away. I surprised all of them. I went off to stay with Sine, my sister, who lived in another village about two hours away, if you traveled by bus. I was in such a state of shock when I finally left that I just couldn't take it any more. Nothing had changed.

When I stayed with Sine, I helped her with the house and her baby. In the evenings, I went to the church there to help the children learn how to sing songs. It was a new church and they were just starting to teach the people about God and Jesus. I had attended church in my village, so I knew many songs and stories to share with them. I told them all about the man who died and came back from the dead.

I stayed with Sine for approximately a year, but I would make frequent visits to see my friends in my home village of Chunyun. I still went to teenager's night once a week when I could manage it.

I saw Chu as often as I could, too. We missed each other a lot. I thought of him all the time and he told me that he thought of me all the time, too. He knew that I had to stay at Sine's house so my parents wouldn't force me to marry Li.

My mother and her girlfriend couldn't make any wedding arrangements because they were unsure of where I would be from one moment to the next.

One day, Chu asked me, "Why don't we run away and get married?"

"Chu, I'm far too young," I said. "If we get married, I will be stuck in one place raising children for the rest of my life, just like my mother. I want to go places and do things. I'm too young to stay home doing the same thing day in and day out. I've watched too many women doing that."

I knew that if I married Chu, I wouldn't have my freedom anymore.

"In a few years," I said, "maybe we could get married. I'm seventeen and I haven't done anything yet. I have to see what I want to do first. Maybe I want to live on the farm and maybe I don't. Right now, we love each other. When you get married and settle down, things can change."

"I understand," Chu said.

But I knew him well enough that I could see by the expression on his face that he was hurting very badly. I think he had been very lonely while I was staying with my sister because we didn't see each other as often as usual. All he knew since the time he was little was my world and likewise, all I knew since the time I was little was his world. I think he was very upset, but he didn't want to hold me back. He was the type of person who didn't want me to do things I did not want to do.

"Right now, we are together and we are having fun," I said. "If we were a married couple, it would not be the same. It would be different. I would be stuck at home raising the children and you would have to work very hard to support the family. We will have to see what the future will hold for us. Maybe in a few years, things will change and we could be together."

Time passed and finally I made the last of my visits then to Chunyun. I had found that nothing had changed with my family.

I went to the country to see Chu, and we were very happy to be with each other. He held my hand.

"I miss you," he said. "I can't get motivated to do things without you being here. I seem to have lost interest in my usual routine. My life has changed without you around. I feel lost and lonely. I spend too many days alone. I'm not used to that. Before, we would do a lot of things together. I used to get up very early in the morning and help my mother with the farm. Now I don't do that."

He figured he had no future without me. He seemed lonely and depressed. It was a tremendous change for him. He had never been outside of the village of Chunyun and he didn't have any desire to leave the farm to go to the city. He was very close with his mother. He did a lot on the farm, and his mother was very dependent on him to do certain chores and to help her out.

"I'm leaving to go to work in Taipei," I said. "I got a job there. It doesn't pay a lot of money, but it will be enough to pay the bills. I will be sharing an apartment with two other girls. You can come and visit me anytime you want to."

I felt badly, but there was not much I could do because I had plans that I wanted to fulfill. My feeling was that he would wait for me, but I didn't want to live there like that anymore. I wanted to live in the city because they had everything there that we didn't have: doctors, dentists, big stores, schools, and opportunities to work outside of the home.

"I would like to come and visit you," he said. "I will see if I could live there with you."

I left once again.

This time, I was headed for the City of Tai Pai. By then we had a small system of public transportation. It took me about five hours by bus to get to Taipei.

When I arrived in Taipei, I went to stay with my girlfriend. I was so emotionally torn apart that I couldn't think straight. I couldn't deal with the pain. I felt betrayed by my parents. They had denied me being with the only man I ever wanted to be with.

I worked and I kept busy to forget.

A few months after I moved to Taipei, Chu took a bus to the city to visit me. He stayed in a hotel nearby. I was happy to see him, but I could tell he was forcing himself to be there.

I tried to encourage him to like the city and hoped that he would. We walked around and I showed him different places that I thought would interest him. Although he tried not to show it, he was very unhappy the whole time he was there. He was not enjoying himself at all, I could tell.

He finally said to me, "I cannot leave the country because my mother needs me on the farm. I have to be there to help my mother because my brother moved out and got married and had children. He doesn't have time to help her the way he used to. She depends on me." Chu was very loyal to his mother.

"I understand, "I said. "You know, I don't think I ever would have left Chunyun except for the fact that my mother was going to force me to marry Li. But I've gotten used to my new life now. I don't have to worry about my parents pushing me to do anything I don't want to do. I like living here in the city, and I am very fond of the other two girls I am living with. It's a different lifestyle for me. This is what I want to do right now. I am free. I work very hard and have long hours, but I am learning to be independent."

Chu stayed in Taipei for four days, but after that, he decided he wanted to go back home to Chunyun. He wasn't enjoying himself.

When it was time for him to leave left Taipei, I decided to take the bus back to Chunyun with him to keep him company. I also wanted to spend more time with him because I was still in love with him.

When we were sitting on the bus, Chu didn't say much. The silence was deafening. I was the only one who was doing the talking. I told him what I hoped to do with my career and my plans to stay in the city. I think he knew that we weren't going to spend too much time together anymore. He didn't feel good at all.

"Maybe we should get all our friends together this weekend," I said to him.

"That's a good idea because a lot of our friends haven't seen you for a long time," he said. "I don't think you should wear any make-up or dress the way you are now, though, because it will have a bad effect on the other girls. They might want to dress and act the way you are. You know, you used to have the most beautiful hair I'd ever seen. I used to love to braid it. I used to love the feel of the long silky strands of your hair. Now, I can't braid your hair anymore. Your hair is nice now, but it is so different. When the other girls see your short hair, I'm afraid they will want to copy you. Don't wear any lipstick when you see them, either."

He was telling me what to do even though he had never done this before. I was surprised. I didn't like the fact that he was suddenly so inflexible.

"I would really like to stay in the city," I said to him. "You should come back again. You were only there for four days. I know it was your first time in Taipei, and that everything was very new to you, but you should really give it another try, Chu."

I took off from work for a week so I could stay in the country with Chu. I thought that we needed to spend some time together in the element that we grew up in. The next day, we went to the lake in the country to try to recapture our feelings for one another so that we could better remember the good times we had had.

"Chu, do you remember the day that I saw my reflection in the water and I thought I looked so ugly?" I asked. "You told me how cute I was and you made me feel better."

"Yes, I remember," he said.

"I remember another time," I said, "when we were here alone swimming and you dove way under the water. You stayed down under the water for a long time and I got scared that you drowned. I kept running back and forth by the lake, looking for you. Soon I was terrified. I didn't even have the dog with me to send him in the water to look for you. I almost ran to get help, but I knew that we were so far away from civilization that by the time I got back, it would be too late for you. I was screaming, 'Chu, Chu. I'm not leaving here. I really care for you. Please come up. I don't want you to die. I want to live with you. Don't die yet. We have so much to do together. I need you. You are the only man I love. I really care for you. Where are you, Chu?'"

"A few minutes later, you appeared from under the water. I said, 'I thought you drowned yourself. I know it's very deep out there. My father always told me not to go near the whirlpool because you can't get out of that current. I thought you were gone forever.'"

"You laughed at me. Then you said, 'I think you care for me.' That was the first time I had ever told you I loved you."

Chu looked at me, but he wasn't sharing my memory. "When I don't see you, do you know how I feel now? I feel sad and upset. Do you understand?" He had a funny look on his face.

"Yes, I understand," I said. Chu still looked very upset.

"When you are not around now," he said, "I come here a lot with the dog to think of you. I dream about the times we spent here. I stay here sometimes for hours on end, and it is often dark when I get back home." Chu had kept my dogs for me when I moved to the city so he would have company.

"Are you mad at me now?" he asked.

"No, I'm not mad at you," I said, "but if something happened to you here, now, I would be the one to get blamed. Your mother knew that we were together. I would not feel good, either. If you had really killed yourself back then, I would have jumped in with you."

When we got ready to leave there, I said, "I'm going to run. See if you can catch me."

I ran and he ran after me. I ran so fast that I could hardly breathe. He caught me and gave me a hug. We held each other's hands and we walked home together.

"My hands are cold," I said.

"I heard somewhere that if you have cold hands," he said, "you have a warm heart, and if you have warm hands, you have a cold heart."

"My heart is always warm for you," I said.

During the week that I was in the village, although I didn't feel that comfortable being around my mother, I stayed at my family's house for part of the time so I could spend time with my father and my sisters. I missed my father during the time I had been away in the city. I missed our times in the country and the long talks we had together. Chu came over daily to help my father with little things that needed to be done. They still got along very well together.

Then Chu and I went to the country to see his parents for a few days. I dragged him to other villages, too, to see how the people lived and to visit the churches. He seemed to enjoy that.

We took public transportation because we didn't own a car and it took at least two hours to get there by bus. We had a good time visiting the people that lived in the villages because they were very different from the people in Chunyun.

Their farming communities were much more established than the farms within my village. They had a lot of flat land and had good soil for farming.

It was interesting to see and it opened my eyes. They sold their vegetables to Tai Pai and other larger villages, but not to Chunyun. They were also active in selling rice and beans and other commodities.

Chu said, "Hotch, maybe we should move here."

"I already told you that I don't want to be a farmer," I said. "I have been doing that my whole life. Farmers work so hard and make so little money. I don't want to live like that anymore."

"When you come home next time, maybe we can come back here and spend more time here," Chu said. "Maybe you could start to like it here. We could find out how they got to be so established."

"Yes, I will, Chu. We can do that," I said.

From time to time, I did go home to visit. On one visit home, I had a nice dress on and wore high heels. One of the girls at the beauty salon had cut my hair so it was a just little bit above my shoulders.

When I saw Chu, he said, "Hotch, you don't look the same as usual. Your hair is so short. You are dressing differently, too, and you look much more cosmopolitan now. You have lipstick on, too. You are living in the big city now and you're not the same girl I used to know."

"But I am the same person inside," I said.

"Don't those high heels hurt your feet?" he asked.

"No, I need to wear these to work so I look professional. I can't look like a farmer. I would be out of place there dressed the way I used to in the country."

"What's happened to you, Hotch?" Chu asked.

"I am going to school now," I said. "I thought you would be proud of me. I'm trying so hard to make a better life for myself. I am learning to be a hairdresser and I am learning to do facials, too. I don't like hairdressing because people are never satisfied with their hair anyway. What I really want to learn to be good at is facials."

"What are facials?" he asked.

"I work on making people's faces look better. I massage people's faces and take out the impurities. The customers can be any age, old, young or in between. I've always liked to work with people. I don't want to be a farmer.

"Your nails have polish on them and are so long that they look like claws."

"Claws?!" I yelled. "I have to polish them so they look pretty. I don't understand you. I have to have my nails looking nice. My appearance is very important in my business. Customers wouldn't come to me if I didn't look nice. They wouldn't let me work on them if I wasn't clean and well dressed. I have to dress appropriately to impress my customers."

"If you say so," Chu said.

"Yes, I enjoy interacting with people very much. I always liked working with people in the church, too. That's why I don't want to get married too young because I want to see different things, Chu. Also, I want to visit other countries."

I could read his face. He seemed lost.

"You have changed your looks totally," he finally said. "I hope you realize that city girls have to be wise in order to protect themselves. People in the country are different. Now, you are dealing more with people and money. You can't necessarily have the same degrees of trust with people in the city. You have to be careful, especially with women. Whatever you do, be careful what direction you go in."

I could tell by his face that he was very sad.

"Yes, you are so right," I said. "My father always told me that, too. It is a very different place there in Taipei than it is here in Chunyun."

I could tell that he could never adapt to the customs of the city. His mother taught Chu certain things from childhood, and he didn't want to learn anything else.

At this moment, I realized that despite our similar backgrounds and the way we grew up, we had become different, very different. A sadness came over me. I knew I could never marry him. I had adapted to my new city environment. He did not have that capacity to change. I remembered that he had told me once that he would never leave his mother.

Even at that time, I knew exactly what I wanted in life.

When I lived in my little village, I saw too much poverty. We struggled hard just for our daily existence. In the country, every day was the same routine. I needed diversity and some excitement. I have always been somewhat adventurous. I always liked to be on the go. I had an inner need to develop myself beyond the little world I left behind in Chunyun.

While there were good things about life in Chunyun—such as living without bills and without stress—it was a very low standard of life. You didn't have to be too motivated. I realized that if I went back to Chunyun, I could live a life of the status quo, and I couldn't accept that.

Besides, I had a strong yearning to see other parts of the world beyond Taiwan. I had a roadmap in my mind, and I was on it and traveling to new and exciting places. I just could not sacrifice my dreams and go back to the farm.

When I was little, I was waiting to grow up so I could go places. I had so many arguments with my mother that I always wanted to get away. I couldn't wait to leave home. I knew that the only way for me to find out about the world was to take action. I was very motivated.

The next time Chu and I got together, we tried once again to get close, like we had been before; but it had been at least five or six months since I had been home to visit him.

He was noticeably different than the last time I had seen him. He seemed so far away.

I felt like I didn't exist in his life anymore. He was not the same young man I once knew. The closeness I felt in the past with him had obviously dissolved. I could feel that he had changed toward me. In some ways, it gave me a sense of relief, and it alleviated the sense of guilt that I had been experiencing.

I felt like he had forgotten me totally. He acted almost as if I was a stranger. My feelings toward him had not changed, though. I hadn't dated anyone else.

"Even though we are not together," I told him, "you are always in my mind."

"I think the same way," he said.

We went to have dinner at my parents' house. My father, Chu and I sat at the dinner table while my mother was in the kitchen. Chu normally had a very good appetite, but that evening he was pensive.

He sat there in deep thought and only played with his food when it came and didn't eat. He kept looking down at the table without giving anyone eye contact. Usually he would smile a lot at me. But tonight he wasn't very communicative, and I was worried about him. He was not himself at all.

My father looked at me and I looked back at him. He knew that Chu was very unhappy, as did I. I didn't know if he was sad about me or angry at me because I was leaving the next day for the city. I didn't know what he had on his mind. I wished I could have been a mind reader.

After dinner, we all sat around for a while talking.

Chu finally said, "I didn't see my mother very much today because I have been with you all day. I should go home soon."

So I walked him outside and we went to sit on top of a nearby rock that was at least thirty feet high. We had to climb up it to get to the top.

We talked for a while. We could see people passing by and we waved to them. It was enjoyable being there with him and looking down at Chunyun.

"Everything down below looks so small," he said. "I see the dog down there. He looks very tiny below."

"Where?" I asked.

"Right there. Do you see him moving?" Chu pointed in the direction of the dog.

"I see him now," I said.

I didn't have any shoes on because my feet hurt. When I lived in the village, I had always gone barefoot. When I moved to the city, I had to wear shoes. My feet were about a size 7 ½ and that was considered to be very large. Most of the other girls wore a size 5 ½. In order to make my feet look small, I bought very small shoes, but they hurt my feet terribly. I was very self-conscious about my feet being so large. I developed awful blisters from wearing such small shoes. My feet would bleed and my toenails would get black and blue. I got large corns that never went away. My toes became permanently gnarled.

Chu asked, "Why don't you buy the right size shoes so your feet don't hurt so much? You can't do that to your feet. You are going to ruin your feet and they will never be the same again."

"You are probably right," I said.

Suddenly he said, "We won't be sitting on this rock again."

"What do you mean?" I asked.

"You have to leave for the city tomorrow."

When I looked at his eyes, he seemed so sad. He was sadder this time than I had ever seen him. We both knew I was leaving the next day, so I figured that was the problem.

"But you will come back to this rock again," he said,

"I might be too old to climb this rock again." I joked.

"Even if you cannot climb up here," he said, "you can always look up and remember tonight."

"I will always remember this rock because I have always climbed up on it since I was a little girl," I said. "When I would come home, as small as I was, I would make my way up here."

Before we climbed down from the rock, I stroked his smooth, thick black hair, and I joked with him again and tried to get him to laugh.

"Let me see if I can pull out some of your hair," I said and tugged on his hair.

"You are pulling my hair too hard, Hotch. Stop it!"

"I don't think your hair is ever going to turn white," I said, "because I can't pull any of it out. You have very strong roots. I would like to see you with white hair and wrinkles some day, though."

"You are never going to see my hair turn white and you will never see me with wrinkles."

"Don't you think you will see my hair turn white and see me with wrinkles someday?" I asked.

"I don't think so," he said.

He didn't explain why he said that and I didn't ask. I thought that he said it because he was not feeling well.

I asked him, "Are you feeling upset because I am leaving for Taipei in the morning?"

"No," was all he said.

He sat there on the rock silently for a long time.

I knew that sometimes he was moody, but this was very peculiar.

"I know you are feeling badly, but you aren't talking to me," I said. "Do you remember when you came to visit me in the city? When we went out one night, I wasn't wearing a bra. Remember you told me that you didn't like the way it looked because people could see the shape of my breasts."

We were far away from my apartment when he noticed, but he made me go home and put a bra on. We had to walk for miles.

"You told me that I shouldn't walk around like that. You told me that if I didn't change, you wouldn't ever walk around with me like that again. Then you told me to never do that again. I didn't get angry, though, even though you were telling me what to do.

After that, I never bought a blouse that was too thin and or too see through."

I did tell myself after that, however, that I was glad I was not with him twenty-four hours a day. After that, when he was with me, I started feeling that I didn't want to be with him. When I was with him, he made me feel uncomfortable.

But when I was not with him, I always missed him and thought of him.

"We better climb down now," he said.

He gradually climbed down and then said, "If you fall, be sure to fall in my arms."

As I came down, he said, "Reach for my arms."

I reached out for his arms and he pulled me toward him.

"You are very light," he said.

"Well, do you want me to come down again so you can see how heavy I really am?" I asked.

"No, we have to go home."

"I'm going to miss you," I said.

He didn't respond.

"I'm going to come back home in a few months. I'll see you then," I said.

Again, he didn't respond.

He walked away from me.

I chased him. "Chu, wait, wait! I have something to tell you. I miss you already!"

I held his hand very tight. "I'm always going to think of you, okay, Chu?" I said.

"I'll see you."

He ran off into the darkness. He had trouble expressing himself when he was sad.

"I'll see you in a few months, Chu."

"Hotch, take care of yourself," he finally said.

That was the last thing he said as he turned around briefly and waved at me. Chu was a very serious person, but he would usually joke around so I figured the relationship was over.

I went home. I didn't feel right about Chu. My father was standing there waiting to talk with me.

"Come here and sit down," he said. "I'm worried about Chu. When he was sitting at the dinner table, I noticed he didn't eat much. He usually has a hearty appetite, but not tonight. I noticed that his eyes looked very sad. That's why I looked at you the way I did at the table. I can tell that he wants to be with you and that he is lost without you. He seemed so unhappy tonight. When you are in the city, he only came here to visit me one time and he seemed disoriented. I have a bad feeling about him."

"Dad, you know that I have changed since I moved to the city. I don't want to stay here and be a farmer. I used to think we had a future together, but I don't think that anymore. In spite of that, a lot of times, I can't go to sleep because I am thinking of him still. I'm leaving here tomorrow and I don't know the exact date that I will be back, but sometime in a few months. Dad, will you talk to Chu when I am away and help him gradually understand? I don't want to hurt him."

"I know what to say," my father said. "I will talk to him when he comes by."

"I will never come back here to live and get married," I said. "You know that I sometimes get sick. They have doctors there in Taipei. They have so many modern conveniences that we don't have here, not to mention all of the opportunities that are available."

"You have to choose what you want to do, Robi. You are very brave. Chu is not as brave as you are. Your mind is very strong. When you make up your mind, no one can change it. Wherever you go and whatever you do, make sure you take the right path. I know you will make it because I taught you to be strong. I treated you to be as tough as if you were a son."

"You did teach me to be strong," I said. "When the tough times come, I always think of you. You always encouraged me to make myself better. You are so different than my mother. You know I always listen to you."

I adored my father. He never put me down the way my mother did.

"Life is up and down," he said. "That's just the way it is. I know you will be fine. We better go to bed now because you have to get up in the morning to take the bus into the city."

I knew that my feelings about Chu would never change as long as I lived. I wished I had known what was in the deepest parts of his mind. None of us had any idea of what was to occur later on.

A few months went by. I went back to the village again. There was a strangeness in the air. I had experienced so much during the past year in Taipei that the village seemed smaller than ever before and more boring than I ever thought.

I went to see my parents. I remember when I walked into the house, my mother looked at me and I know she must have seen by the look on my face how unhappy I was to be there.

But there was a strong sense of guilt on her face that no mask could cover, even though she tried to gloss it over with niceties.

"I'm glad you are home," she said. "You look good. We miss you here. I just cooked some vegetables and beans. Your father went to visit your aunt. I want you to sit down. Can you stay for a while?"

"Okay," I said.

"I have so many things to tell you," she said, "I really don't know where to start. I don't how to express myself very well. When I was growing up, my mother spoiled me a lot. She gave me everything I wanted. I learned to boss a lot of people around. I didn't know how to discipline you properly. I had all of you children just left and right. I was too busy. I had no idea of how to take care of you children. You were very different, too. You were much more mature than the rest of the children. You went out to work early on. I remember when you started working for a quarter as an entire day's wage. I know I chased you out of the house. I realized a lot of things after you left for the city. Then I knew it was too late. It was a very painful thing for me to learn. I know I never really took the time to be a mother to you because you were so active. I only know that my sister had one boy and she wanted a girl very badly. Out of the four girls, she liked you the best. I thought you should go live with her. I was worried about raising the five of you and providing for all of you. Our boy was about five years old and I thought it was a good time for you to go live with your aunt so the two of you could grow up together. I was only seventeen and very young when I married your father. I was very busy and I had each of you children one right after the other. I thought it would be the best thing to make you go live with my sister, but I was wrong. I was also wrong to try to arrange your marriage. I didn't realize that you and Chu were so much in love. I want to know if you can forgive me for all of this."

"Don't feel bad," I said. "I know I am more active than my sisters. I know I am always restless, and most of the time you can't handle me and I drive you crazy. Not only that, but I am so young and yet I know what I want. If there is something that I want, I go after it. During all of these years, you never taught me very many things. I knitted sweaters and I sewed a lot, all by myself, and you got angry with me for trying. I am seventeen now, and I don't want to live here and become a farmer's wife because I know what that involves, and it's not for me. I want something different for my life. Maybe change is good and maybe it is not. Sometimes I am afraid to change, but either way, the only way I know is to do it. I can't just talk about it."

"Now that you live in the city," my mother said, "you have to work very hard to take care of your appearance, your hair, your make-up and your clothes because you have to fit in with the crowd. You have been skinny all of your life. Maybe you should gain some weight and fill out a little bit. Don't wear short skirts. Wear long skirts so that you can hide how skinny you are. You have a cute face and you have beautiful eyes. All you need to do is gain a little weight. If you get married and have a baby, don't breast feed because one day your breasts will hang. It looks awful and it doesn't matter even if you exercise, your breasts won't be firm and won't come back into shape. Where I came from we didn't have any cow's milk or goat's milk. We made milk from rice, but this was a time consuming process. Then, when babies are about five or six months old, you start to feed them a little bit of pureed vegetables and rice noodles."

"I think you realize that in Taipei," she continued, "it is probably not a good idea to act like you live in the country. You should go to modeling school, where they will teach you how to walk, talk, dress and match your shoes to your outfit. If you look a little bit better than other girls, it's to your advantage. If you think you are going to slip out of the house looking slovenly, you will probably see someone you know when you least expect it. When you start to buy clothes, buy two dresses so you will have a change. Try to go to a dressmaker so your clothes fit your body perfectly. When you go to a tailor, you might be able to get a dress made in the same day. In the city, everyone watches her weight, so you have to do the same thing. It's very competitive. You should always look good no matter what your age and no matter how bad you feel. People in the city are very observant. Don't wear a lot of make-up. With less you look better and more natural."

She had just been going on and on.

"Not only that," she said, "but I have to tell you something else, so you might want to prepare yourself for some very bad news. When you were away in the city, they found Chu."

"What do you mean, they found Chu?" I asked. My heart was pounding. I felt an enormous sense of fear rushing through my veins. I stared coldly into my mother's eyes. Seconds that felt like minutes passed by. The room was cold. I felt a chill.

My mother looked at me. Choking, she said, "By the time his mother found his body, it was too late. They aren't sure how he did it, but it looks like he took something, maybe some sort of poison."

I screamed at her, "No, that can't be true!"

Then I ran outside as fast as my legs could carry me. My thoughts were a blur and my heart started racing. I felt as if I was strangling to death. I couldn't breathe and tears were streaming down my face so hard that I could barely see where I was going. My mother's words about Chu's death were playing over and over in my mind.

I was in a state of disbelief, so the only thing I knew to do was to run to a place by the river where Chu and I used to go together.

But there was no sign of him there.

I sat down and stayed there for a while. I began talking to him. I said, "Chu, this can't be true. Tell me you didn't really do this."

I became angry and upset with him. I shouted at him, "You coward! How could you do this! You always told me to be strong and now look at what you've done to yourself. I can't believe this. Please answer me, Chu."

I heard only the silence of the night.

I said, "You are hiding from me again. Please come out."

I sat there for a long time crying.

"This time," and I began to stutter, "I...I...don't think...I don't think you are coming out..."

Then I sobbed uncontrollably...

Visions of the two of us swimming and laughing ran through my mind. I drifted back to one day when we were right there by the river. We had no mirrors where I lived at that time because the area was so rural. I looked into the river. All at once, for the first time, I saw my reflection in the water. I said to Chu, "Oh, my God. Look at my reflection in the water. Chu, I'm ugly. I have big eyes and a skinny face and long hair."

I could remember that night as if it were yesterday when we went walking to the river with the dogs and the full moon was out. I felt very close to him.

I remembered how we used to joke around together. When I was sad, he knew how to make me laugh.

That night he said, "No, you are cute. Don't say you are ugly. It's not true. Your eyes, your skin and your hair are all beautiful."

He pulled my long hair back from my face and he said, "Now, Hotch, look again in the water so you can see your full face."

I leaned forward and looked at my reflection in the water. I started to believe his words because he seemed to believe what he said.

Then he said, "Let's go. Don't worry about that. The water does not really give you a true reflection. One day we'll go into the city and I'll buy you a mirror. Then you can see how beautiful you really are."

A black bird flew overhead, making cawing sounds. It startled me out of my pleasant memories of Chu and brought my mind back to the moment. The sad news began to really sink in.

I realized that Chu and I would never be able to go to the city to buy the mirror. We would never go anywhere together, ever again.

I remembered how he had softly pulled my hair back that day. That moment was gone forever.

I sat there for a long time.

The sun began to set. It was almost dark.

The news of Chu's suicide devastated me.

Apparently, he had become very depressed after he last saw me and he didn't want to live anymore. I had had no idea he was so unhappy.

Something drew me to his house in the county.

I ran there. I saw that his house was wide open, although this was not unusual because no one locked their doors in the country. I went into his room and there were no signs of him there. I didn't see any of his familiar belongings.

I wondered where everyone was, but I was so upset that I didn't feel like seeing anyone anyway.

I sat down in the chair in his room for a long time, just thinking. I could still smell Chu's scent there. The world seemed to stop because Chu was gone. My mind was reeling. The pain was indescribable. My heart sank in despair for my loved one.

I walked around outside and picked some flowers. I took the flowers to the river spot where we used to go, and I threw them into the water as a memorial. I said a prayer for his soul, that he would have peace and know how much I cared for him while he was alive.

To this day I think of the possibilities that could have transpired with Chu and me. I only wish I could have been there to stop him. We could have run away together. I knew that we loved each other, but I didn't think he would take such drastic measures into his own hands. I didn't know that he was so intensely involved over me on that level the last time I saw him.

He knew I wasn't going to marry Li no matter what, but I think my move to the city upset him more than I knew. It all must have been too traumatic for him.

I remember a conversation I had with his mother when she told me how sensitive he was, and it was true, he was sensitive and very serious, too. I now realize that the only way he could stop thinking and worrying about me was to take his own life. He was too sensitive.

In the Taiwanese culture, it is our custom not to be too open with our feelings. We don't express ourselves outwardly very easily and we generally keep our sadness to ourselves.

Later on, my mother told me that they buried Chu's body in the country where they found him. That's where his family had their farm and that's where we spent most of our time together.

I still somehow tend to blame myself for what happened. I have an enormous guilt and sadness that will stay with me forever.

Every time I sit someplace to watch a sunset, I get very emotional because I see Chu's handsome face in the sun and he is smiling at me. Sometimes, I ignore the sunset. Many times I just sit there and cry.

After I found out the horrible news about Chu's death, my health rapidly deteriorated. I expect that was due to all the stress. I could not and never will forget what happened. My body just shut down.

After that, my feelings changed and I never felt happy for a long time. I didn't have anyone to talk with, either. Toyoko was gone. I was very lonely. I'm sure that everything would have been different had she remained alive because she was one person I could always share my feelings with.

When this happened—after you love someone the way I loved Chu—everything changed.

After that, my stomach bothered me terribly. I could no longer take a bus because I would get nauseous. When I came to the States, I couldn't ride a car without getting sick. I could only drive for about a half hour and then I would feel awful. I never could have a fixed schedule for my meals.

Sometimes, I wouldn't eat dinner. I would starve myself and go to sleep on an empty stomach. When I did eat, I had pain in my stomach. I couldn't keep food down. I thought I had ulcers. I had to hold my stomach while I was sleeping, or I should say, when I could sleep. Sometimes when I even looked at food, it made me nauseous.

After Chu died, my mind was not working like it had before. I was not motivated to do a lot of things I had done before. I didn't have the same strength.

I knew that I could never go back to where I had been before, to where he had been. He would never be there for me the way he had been.

I had terrible insomnia for a long time. I could not stop blaming myself. I could not block it out of my mind for the longest time.

My roommates asked me what was wrong with me. I never exposed my personal life with them. I kept my feelings to myself. One day three of my girlfriends took me out to dinner. I told them not to order too much food for me because I had eaten a late lunch. I only ate rice and vegetables.

One of the girls told me that something must be very wrong with me because I always seemed to have a stomach ache. They were all worried about me.

I used to get up very early in the morning. One particular morning, I couldn't get out of bed. My roommates took me to see the doctor. I was very weak. The doctor looked at my eyes. He told me that I needed to have vitamin B-12 injections once a week and that I had to eat. He gave me other vitamins to take, too. He asked me if I worked long hours or if I was sleeping. I told him that I was very stressed out. He told me to stay home from work until I got my strength back again.

I had a friend that I met at the beauty salon where I worked. She always looked after me. She told me that I was too thin and that I did not look good. My girlfriend began to get very worried about my health.

She said, "You better take your health seriously because if you don't, it could be dangerous for you. Something is bothering you, I can tell. If you want to talk with me, I won't tell anybody. You can tell me if you want to."

I told her a little bit about what had happened.

"I hope you can snap out of this," she said. "You are in a lot of pain. I will do anything I can to help you. The best advice I can give you is to keep yourself busy and try not to re-live the pain. I know that is easier said than done. It is painful, but life must go on without your friend. You have too much to live for, and since I have worked with you and gotten to know you, I know that you are an individual who has many dreams to fulfill. You must be strong, the way your father taught you. You will get over this. Only you can do this for yourself. I know it is very hard to get over the painful memories. I will be there for you as much as I can. The first thing you need to do is to get some sleep. Take the vitamins the way the doctor told you. It is going to take a while, but you can do it."

From that point on, I took her advice.

I kept myself as busy as possible. I went places with my friends. We went to see funny movies. On the weekends, we would go places where there were lots of people. We would go sightseeing and we did a lot of walking. Often when we were out walking, we would stop at a little café and have a snack on the way home.

Sometimes I would think that I might not be able to recuperate. I had very little strength, emotionally and physically, but I eventually came to the point where I could relax and I could keep my food down. My girlfriends were very helpful as they kept me busy.

One time my girlfriend said to me, "We are all going to get dressed up and go into the city. You're going to put on a pretty dress and get your hair and your nails done."

I finally decided to go to a shoe store and buy shoes that fit. I had to special order the shoes because my foot size was 7 ½ and this was unheard of. All of the other women wore size 4 ½ to 5 ½. It took about a week to get my shoes, but I will never forget how comfortable they felt.

"There is a nice place we are going to go," my girlfriend said, "that has music and dancing. You don't have to dance. You can just sit there and watch. The main thing you have to do is to relax and try to have a good time."

My girlfriends and I went shopping. They wanted to help me pick out a new outfit. I had finally overcome my self-consciousness about my feet being so big.

We went to the club and while I was sitting there, I thought to myself that I had to change my feelings and my thinking. I told myself that I had to stop beating myself up over this. I knew I was still young and that there must be something else out there waiting for me.

The other girls all danced and I sat there and just relaxed and watched everyone having fun. It helped me when I got out.

Chu would always hold a special place in my heart, but I realized the world hadn't stopped spinning and that life had to go on for me.

One day back in Chunyun all of the villagers got together and had a meeting. My father was then chief of the village, and he made decisions for a lot of people. At the meeting they decided to do away with arranged marriages because so many young people had taken their lives. The adults decided to stay out of the children's relationships. Some people liked the decision, but many others did not like it at all. After all, this was all that the villagers knew all their lives. It was custom, but it had become counterproductive.

After what happened with Chu, I didn't want to get close to any other boys. I really loved Chu very deeply. My parents never understood because they didn't want to. They couldn't relate to me because their marriage had been arranged. Some people who had had their marriages arranged were happy, but there were very few.

It's a difficult thing to explain what happened to me, but for a very long time after that I kept an emotional distance from the opposite sex. I didn't want to be separated from anyone I loved again, so I avoided forming emotional ties with any boys. That was what I called "playing it safe."

Even now, when I am really attracted to someone, I back away from that person. To this day I am unable to form close attachments to men. I never got over the psychological pain of this experience. It will probably stay with me for the rest of my natural life. However, I will always have the memories of the things Chu and I shared together and the significance of the little gestures of love, however innocent, with which we displayed our true and deep affections toward one another. Even though our relationship was not sexual, because we were very young, it was true love, and the memories still remain with me today. I will never forget him.

After Chu's death I didn't feel like I had a purpose in life anymore. I was very depressed. I became very sick and had serious menstrual difficulties. I was bleeding non-stop and felt like I was bleeding to death. The only person I had told was my girlfriend. I would not tell my parents because I did not want them to worry.

Finally I went to see one doctor. Then I went to a few other doctors. One gynecologist was supposed to be the best.

That doctor said that I had to have an operation, which he performed. When the doctor performed surgery on my stomach, he found some sort of growth that had to be removed. After the surgery I had to have several transfusions, but they ended up giving me trouble because I contracted hepatitis. The doctors over there were not as skilled at that time as they are now.

Right after the doctor opened me up, I couldn't open my eyes for along time. They thought that I was gone. I was in a coma and I could not get up for four or five days. They almost buried me.

During this time, I could hear my father calling out to me. All I could heard was his voice saying, "Get up. Get up."

Finally, I began to open my eyes and when I did, I remember feeling sad because my father was not there.

My close girlfriend was, though, and finally I was able to get out of bed. Strangely enough, I thought I had just come from the operating room. After the surgery I was so weak that I not able to work for two months.

In some respects in those days, my mother helped me. She had given me good advice about my appearance. She told me to watch my weight, watch my diet, and not to get fat. She told me to watch the way I dress.

She said, "When you go out, put your handkerchief in your purse. You don't even need money."

This worked, too. Whenever we went out, we were always treated by the men.

CHAPTER II
Marriage to my Husband

The war had ended and Taiwan was a free country when I decided to leave Taipei.

I first met my husband at a place where I worked which sold homemade wooden furniture. He was an American citizen and he came there looking for furniture shortly after his tour of duty at the American Embassy in Taiwan.

After two years of dating, we married. Our first ceremony took place in the American Embassy in Taiwan. When we got married there, about twenty other couples got married at the same time. When the official pronounced us man and wife, he told us to bow to our spouses. By mistake, I bowed in the wrong direction toward another man who was getting married to another woman.

We then had to have a second ceremony, which took place in Taipei at the town hall, to certify that I was a full American citizen.

At the time of the second ceremony, my daughter was already about a year old. She and I had to get many vaccinations for the entire year leading up to our entering the United States. This was required by law in order for us obtain American passports that stated that we were coming here permanently, and not just to visit.

Just as my daughter turned a year old, I was about 27 or 28 and I contracted a very bad case of hepatitis. I was in the hospital for two months. My husband took me to the best hospital in Taipei, where all of the doctors had been educated in the United States.

Before I had hepatitis, I had a dream that someone stabbed my stomach. It was very painful. Maybe it was a warning, but I ignored the dream.

My bones and my muscles were achy with the disease and I was very tired. At first, I told myself that I was probably just tired. Then I got headaches, too. My back and my shoulders ached the most.

Finally one day I went to the doctor with my husband. The doctor checked my blood and checked me all over. After the blood tests came back, the doctor kept me in his office. He told me I had hepatitis. When my husband came into the room, the doctor shook his head in a "no" motion to let my husband know he didn't think I was going to make it. He didn't think I saw him shake his head like that, but I did.

I was very sick. I threw up all of the time for no apparent reason, even when I had no food in my stomach. If I merely drank water, it would come right back up too. It was awful. I lost so much weight that I dropped to ninety pounds.

That first doctor I saw gave me an intravenous tube 24 hours a day, but I don't think he knew how to treat hepatitis properly. My husband got upset with this doctor and hired another doctor, reputed to be the best doctor in Taipei. He too had been trained in the United States.

I ended up going through quite a few doctors before I found one who could treat me properly. I had awful symptoms. I became jaundiced. I was constantly throwing up. For a long time I couldn't keep any food down.

In the hospital, the doctor gave me at least twelve different kinds of vitamins. I had actually had the disease for six months prior to my being diagnosed. It wasn't until I became critically ill that I realized I was so sick. My system had been able to fight it off for a long time, but then it finally wore me down.

At one point, I had to say to myself, "I'm going to make it." Then, when I had been there for about four weeks, I started to improve a little bit each day.

When I was in the hospital during this time, there was an earthquake. The walls cracked all around me. I watched it happen. I remember it was in the afternoon around 2:00 because I had just been served dessert. Many of the patients ran outside because they were afraid and panicked, but almost everyone who ran out of the hospital got killed because the building fell on top of them. Fortunately, my father had always taught me to go stand in the doorway if we had an earthquake.

It took me a long time, about a year, to recuperate from the hepatitis, but I was only in the hospital for eight weeks, although that seemed like a very long time, too. When I left the hospital, I had to have a blood test every week for the next month or so to make sure the hepatitis was gone.

You have to really take care of yourself and discipline yourself during this kind of illness. If you really watch yourself, you can make it. If you don't watch yourself, you might not be able to make it.

The recuperation period was very slow. Once, when I ate raw fish, my husband screamed and screamed at me. I would not touch any raw food after this, even to this day. My husband had a good heart, but there were still a lot of things that were not right.

When I had hepatitis, there was a very strict and special diet I had to follow. I had to eat very mild foods: rice, vegetables, sweet potatoes, chicken, decaffeinated green tea. I couldn't smoke. I could have no liquor, no sweets, no oil, no fried food, no raw food, no fish, no crustaceans, no shellfish, and no coffee.

Until my husband screamed at me, if had fish, it had to be fresh to begin with, and then it had to be cooked well. I could never eat raw food. Everything I ate had to be cooked. I couldn't eat any leftovers. I couldn't eat cheese. I couldn't eat mushrooms because they are so high in bacteria. I couldn't drink alcohol for at least the next two years. I couldn't eat any hot and spicy foods because they irritated my system. When I was recuperating, I could never go out to eat because I didn't know how they prepared the food.

I couldn't stand cold weather. When it was cold out, I had to make sure I was all bundled up. I slept a lot. I had to boil all my own water. I had to stay on this diet for a year or more, or else the hepatitis could have come back. I couldn't kiss anyone on the mouth because it could be highly contagious. I had to take a lot of vitamins and I constantly went to a nutritionist and took what he prescribed.

My last doctor told me I was very strong to have made it through this hepatitis. A lot of people don't make it. It took me two years to recuperate, and then I still had to watch my diet and everything I did. Just because I felt better, I still had to always take extra care of myself.

I still have to have blood tests.

After that I always paid attention to my dreams, too. Sometimes dreams are indicators of what is going to happen in the future. Sometimes dreams come true. That's why dream interpretation is an important issue and worth paying attention to.

I was about 28 years old when my husband and I first arrived at Los Angeles Airport with our baby girl. From Los Angeles we went to Hollywood, California.

That first night I watched television in the motel room. I waited up all night for the color to come on the television because the television had only been in black and white. But it never turned to color.

The next day I went to the stores to do some shopping. I went to some clothing stores and looked around and also went to some shoe stores. I was so happy to find out that they had my size 7½ shoe in stock. Not only that, they had up to size 12.

I went to a local dress shop and was trying to learn about American culture. There was a lady there who was about 60 years old. I spoke English, not very well, but I asked her if she worked there. In Taiwan, women stayed at home and worked. They did not go outside to work.

Here I saw many women over 60 years old who were working in businesses. I told myself that I had better do something for myself and find a profession because, when I saw all of these women working, I realized that I had to look for a job too. After that, I always thought I had to work.

That second night I found out that on a TV, color and black and white were different. I never told my husband I had stayed up so late the previous night because I did not want him to make fun of me.

When I first watched television in California, my favorite movie was about Tarzan. I just loved to watch it because it reminded me of my native country, which I had become a little bit homesick for. The film had a lot of animals in it that I never seen before, and I could watch that same movie over and over again and never get tired of it.

We stayed in Hollywood for about two weeks.

Then we went to Bridgeport, Connecticut, and lived in my mother-in-law's house for approximately one year. We went there because my husband's mother was ill.

My husband had one sister, named Helen, and one brother, named Chubby. They lived there, too. The house was not big and it was crowded. There were six of us living there with only one bathroom.

I was uncomfortable living at my mother-in-law's. My mother-in-law asked too many questions. She wanted to know all our business. One day she asked me why she did not ever see me ever kiss my husband. I told her that in Taiwan, I was taught not to kiss a man in front of anyone because that was a private affair between a man and a woman. A woman was not supposed to do that.

My daughter was only two years old and she was very active, but it was too crowded for her there. I was so unhappy. I felt like I wanted to pick up my things and move back to Taiwan, but I tried to be patient for my daughter's sake. I kept telling my husband that we had to leave the United States.

On the second day that we were there, I can remember hearing news that rocked the country. It was June 7th, 1968. United States Senator Robert Kennedy gave his victory speech in the ballroom of the Ambassador Hotel in Los Angeles, California, after winning the California primary. After his speech Senator Kennedy was assassinated by Sirhan Sirhan.

While we lived there, my husband's brother, Chubby, was always very nice and always gave presents to my daughter. Chubby took care of my mother in law, he cooked, and he cleaned the house.

Sometimes my husband's sister, Helen, and I would talk. One day she asked me many questions about religion. She told me that she never went to church, although she wanted to.

Helen did not get along with my mother-in-law. My mother-in-law wanted Chubby to stay home because she wanted him to be there to help her, but she wanted Helen to move out. Helen was not ready to move out, though.

She was seventeen years old when she first started working. Helen was young and very inexperienced about life. She did not have any profession. She was a nice girl, and she was very quiet. She was cute, but she had never dated at all when she was in her teens. She was innocent.

Helen had always stayed at home, but now my mother-in-law wanted her to move out.

Helen did finally move out when she was about twenty-six years old. She was chased out by my mother-in-law. I was very busy at the time trying to get out from there myself.

I knew there would be no way Helen was going to have an easy time of it out in the world. She moved to California, but she had hardly any money in her pockets.

She had only been in California about a year when my mother-in-law got a phone call from the police department. My mother-in-law and my husband went to California to identify the body. It was Helen.

After that my mother-in-law blamed herself. She thought it was her fault for making Helen move out at such a young age. My mother-in-law was never right after that. She felt bad.

When a young girl is out there on her own, it can be very difficult for her. When she runs into problems, she has no one to turn to. People out there are not always kind. If you need something, people aren't always helpful. You should never make your daughter move out when she is not ready. She won't have enough life experience, enough schooling or any profession. When a young girl is by herself out there, it is too dangerous. If you do send her out, it can come back to haunt you. Look what happened to Helen.

I think Helen knew that she was not going to have a long time here on this earth because of all the questions she had asked me about religion.

The first day I went shopping in a grocery store in America I was shocked by all of the food. We didn't have any grocery stores in Taiwan. I started buying all kinds of things when I went to the grocery store because I had never seen so much food like that in my whole life. My eyes opened so wide. I saw all the meat, the fresh fruit, the vegetables.

Every time I went to the store, I would buy so much food that my husband would yell at me, "Who are you going to feed with all of that food?!"

I used to just hang around the grocery store because I was intrigued with the amount of fresh fruit and vegetables. This became my kick. I wouldn't necessarily buy anything, I would just walk through and look. My eyes stayed so wide open because I could not believe what I saw. I was fascinated.

Once when we were traveling, I went to a grocery store. I bought seven different fruits and went and sat in the car until I had eaten all the fruit. But my eyes were too big for my stomach.

I got so sick that I had to be taken to the emergency room. They had to pump my stomach out. My stomach was not right for a long time after that, and I looked terribly pale and yellow. To this day, I cannot eat fruit. Every time I look at fruit, I still get sick. My daughter never forgot this, and she still talks about it today.

After we had lived in Bridgeport a few months, I visited New York City for the first time with my husband and my little girl for a family day trip. I was very disappointed. I had envisioned New York City as a beautiful and perfectly clean metropolis, but it wasn't that way at all. I saw garbage bags on the streets.

I was startled. This was in the late 1960's after the hippy revolution had begun. The culture of the United States had been transformed with the advent of Dr. Timothy Leary and the discovery and widespread use of LSD. This was completely foreign to me and completely opposite to the only culture I had known. In Taiwan we did not have any hippy revolution or any drugs that I ever heard of or knew of.

I was very unhappy then, and I had a strong desire to go back to Taiwan.

In Taiwan, everybody would get dressed up after 6:00 p.m. The women would wear their expensive jewelry. They would go to the hairdresser every week. We would go to movies, restaurants, and nightclubs at night. The women's dress, hair, and make-up were very important to them.

At 12:00 midnight, or at least by 1:00 in the morning, everyone would go home. They would not stay out the way they do here. When they make movies in Taiwan, they don't show sex, violence or drugs. They don't want to expose the children or the society to this sort of thing. They are very strict there.

Every time I would go out, my husband would say, "What time will you be home?"

If I said "three hours," he would say that I'd better be sure that I was home in three hours. If I was late, he would start screaming, "Where have you been? Who have you been with?"

If I was on the phone, he would say, "Who's that?"

Sometimes when I would go out, he would follow me.

I finally said to myself, "This marriage is not working. This is not a marriage. I'm in a jungle with an animal."

My daughter was only three years old, and I used to drag her with me to buy groceries. I didn't have a driver's license yet, so we would have to take a bus to go to the supermarket. My husband was working. It would be raining and we would both get soaking wet. I felt sorry for her because she was so little. She shouldn't have been dragged everywhere.

One day I had a talk with myself and I realized that I did not need my husband any more. My husband was not very industrious and he didn't want to move our family in a forward direction.

I became very unhappy. I couldn't eat and I lost a lot of weight. I had migraine headaches. I was taking pills to go to sleep and pills to get up in the morning.

I don't think he had enough money to move out himself. I never asked him how much money he had in the bank. In China a woman never asked questions. She never asked how much money a man had in the bank.

I decided to find a job there so I could develop my occupation.

One day I said to my husband, "Let's sit down. I want to talk with you."

I told him I wanted to leave, but I asked him which one of us was going to move out. I told him that one of us had to move. He said that he had thought he was important to me.

Then he asked, "Where are you going to go with that kid? You don't know too much English."

He underestimated me because he thought I could not live without him.

I had a neighbor who had a daughter who was the same age as my daughter. When I went to work, she would baby sit my daughter and they would play together. She and I became good friends.

I think her husband drank a lot. They had an argument one night. They always had arguments. He was not a bad person when he was sober, but when he was drinking, he was like an animal. He got very angry with her that night, and he threw something at her, but it hit their daughter in the face. She had to go to the emergency room and get twenty stitches. After that, he didn't argue with his wife anymore.

One day I told her that I was getting a divorce. She wanted to know if I could take care of myself. I told her that I was taking care of myself then and that I paid all of the bills. When my husband got his paycheck, I said, he would take the money and buy drinks for everyone.

She told me that she was afraid to leave her husband because she had never gone out to work before. She didn't think she could survive without him because she needed someone to pay the bills. She told me that she couldn't do what I was doing and told me that I had guts.

Since I knew I was leaving my husband, I began searching for an apartment. Every time I found a nice apartment, the landlady would tell me that she wouldn't take children or dogs. People would say that they loved children and dogs, but that they did not want to rent to people with children and dogs.

I felt like getting a plane ticket and going back to Taiwan. However, I knew that a lot of people would love to be in my place. It had taken me so long to get my passport and my visa, and now, I told myself, I was lucky to be here. I wanted to make a good life for my daughter and myself.

I was not really myself at all, though. Part of me was sad then and the other part was lonely.

I was experiencing a great deal of difficulty finding an apartment, but finally I found a small two bedroom apartment. It was not fancy, but it was okay. The neighborhood was safe.

I moved out of my mother-in-law's house, left my husband, and took my baby girl with me. It was about a year after we moved to the United States.

The reality hit me that I was finally independent, but a wave of fear came over me. I was afraid that I might get sick and might not be able to pay my bills. When you are alone and have no one, it is scary. No matter how much I had to do without, I always had food in the refrigerator for my daughter and me.

I got three different jobs.

I worked at one barbershop doing nails. At first I used to drag my daughter with me to work because I could not afford a babysitter. I did not have a license to cut hair yet. Then I worked at another barbershop cutting hair on a part-time basis, and I had quite a few clients from working there. I worked for myself, too, and met clients to cut their hair at my home. I made one room my office. I would make house calls, as well, to cut women's hair. I was also working at a spa doing facials. They cost $7.00 in those days.

I was working seven days a week and long hours so I could save my money to get a car. My neighbor was now watching my daughter. I was paying all of the bills, the rent, the babysitter. I was buying all the food.

After I was finally settled in my new apartment, I went to see a lawyer. I told him that I wanted to get a legal separation. He put the papers through. For a long time, I couldn't get a divorce because my husband would not agree. The only way I was able to finally get a divorce was when "no fault" divorce came into existence. I had been separated for at least ten years before I could get that divorce.

My daughter and I stayed at our first apartment and then, later on, I got a bigger apartment so I could work more easily at home and spend time with my daughter.

I became sort of an old maid. I went into a state of shock. My hair started turning gray. Then it all began to fall out. This was the effect that that stress had on me. I thought my hair would never grow back again, but it did although it took a year for it all to grow back in.

My husband would make up things against me to tell others. He told his family that I only wanted to marry him because I wanted to come to the United States and become a citizen.

I would never have married him if I hadn't loved him.

I met a friend at night school who was from Czechoslovakia. We got along together very well. We would go fishing a lot. We caught fish and I would take them home and cook them.

I was with him for two years and we talked about getting married. We got along very well. He had dark hair and was tall, slim, very handsome, very romantic, and fun. He wrote to his mother about me and she sent me a handkerchief that I still have.

As soon as he started learning to speak more English, we started to argue. We fought about my daughter. He did not get along with her, but I think he was only jealous.

That was the only thing wrong with our relationship, but it was a big deal to me. I had to put my daughter first. I realized I had to break up with him. Things could have been good with us, except for that. I didn't feel right for a quite a while and I remained very upset.

After I broke up with this man, I missed him so much that I didn't date for a very long time.

That was my last real romance until, after a long time, I finally met someone very special whom I love and cherish. If you have romance, it can change your life. If you have someone there for you, it can help you forget your past relationships. Remember, it doesn't matter how old you are. You are never too old to have romance in your life. It makes you feel vibrant, as if you are young again. It makes your day go by faster. It makes you happier.

It was not until after I broke up with my husband that I myself began to develop as a person. I started attending night school and I studied for my American citizenship. Seven months later I took the test in Bridgeport and passed.

My husband and I had only lived together for about two years in America. The government didn't count the time that we lived together as man and wife in Taiwan. I could have gotten my citizenship if I had waited out one more year with him here. I didn't know that or otherwise I would have stayed with him that other year. Because we had split up, I couldn't get my citizenship for five years.

It wasn't until this time that I started to feel happy. I had started to make a little money and I began to feel a little bit independent since I first arrived here. I had started to put down roots in a culture that had originally seemed very strange and frightening to me.

I started attending the Sherwood Beauty School in Bridgeport, Connecticut. I had to take my daughter to the beauty school with me because I did not have and could not afford a babysitter then. I became acquainted with a lot of girls at the beauty school, and I began to make friends. This too helped me adjust to being here. One of the girls at the beauty school, Linda, became my best friend at that time although there were actually three of us altogether who used to hang around with each other: Linda, Susan and me.

I used to go out a lot with the other girls from work, too, and when we did, we would all put on nice suits and dresses so men would respect us. We used to have a good time. When we dated, we would all go out together and our dates would buy dinner for all of us.

We used to take turns with each man. If we went to dance, one man would have to take all of us with him. If he wanted to be close with one of us, the rest would stay our distance and meet again before we all went home.

One time I met a guy who was much younger than I was and he gave me his credit card so I could go shopping. He had a good job and he made a lot of money, but he didn't get along with my daughter, so I stopped seeing him.

When she had been in high school, my friend Linda had become involved with a man and had dated him steadily for two years. They were doing very well together before he left to serve in the Viet Nam War. She really loved him.

Then he went to the war. All the years he was in Vietnam, she waited for him to come home so they could start a family together. She saved all her money, and she believed that he was going to marry her when he came back from the war because he had promised her that he would.

When he returned from Vietnam, he smoked a lot of marijuana, drank a lot of alcohol, and smoked a lot of cigarettes. He didn't want to do anything else. He just wanted to hang around. He didn't work and he did not value her anymore.

She had thought she had known this man very well.

They finally arranged to get married in a small, private ceremony. That day she rode in the car with me. Her mother and my daughter went to the church in another car by themselves. We all arrived there about 7:00 p.m. and then we waited for about three hours for her boyfriend. Unfortunately for Linda, he never showed up.

She never heard from him again.

He must have known he couldn't take care for her. He couldn't keep a job.

He was never the same person after he came home, but she loved him very much. No matter what, she still wanted him.

After that, everywhere she went, she was always looking for him.

One night we went to a party, and she had a lot to drink. We were going home in my car. I was driving. Suddenly she tried to commit suicide by jumping out of my car. I just managed to stop her.

I took her to her father's house and he took care of her because she was no longer able to function. Linda was so beautiful and so smart, but she got so sick. She turned into a vegetable. Her father continued to take care of her. During all of those years, she still thought this guy would snap out of it and come back and marry her.

Why did she have to let that guy do that to her? She threw her life away for him and he could care less. Why are people like that?

At the time she was only twenty-two years old. Now she is over forty and in the same vegetative state she was in before. She could never get herself right after that happened to her. You can see what love and a broken relationship can do to a person.

My other girlfriend was Susan. She got married and she was happy. No story.

It took me about four years part-time to get my certificate from Sherwood Beauty School.

Generally, I was happy there, but the other girls working there were doing a lot of marijuana because the beauty school was stressful. The instructor and the owner gave us a hard time because they wanted us to do so well. The girls told me to smoke with them to help me relax. I said I wouldn't because I did not want to be wishy-washy. I told them I did not need to smoke pot because I felt as if I was already "there."

Not only that, but I couldn't spend the money to do that stuff.

We would go out on weekends sometimes, the three of us, Linda, Susan and I, the three musketeers. I told the girls, "Take a dollar in your pocketbook just in case anything happens," just like my mother said to me. Once three guys took us out for breakfast after midnight.

After I got my certificate, I was so afraid I would not get a job and was so nervous that I could not sleep at night. I was a little down and crying. I thought that no one was going to give me a job.

I found a couple of jobs part-time. Sometimes I worked in the evening, too. I was so happy that I made my own money. I was paying my own bills. I felt like a new person. I was able to breathe. I was praying every night and I said "thank you" to him.

My neighbors told me that they could not do what I was doing and that I had a lot of guts. I moved to a little bit bigger place so that I could work at home. I went to night school. Weekends and evenings, I worked at home.

I bought a car a year later.

I had the money saved to buy a car, but I was afraid to drive. One day I called the driving school. I went to take my test and the guy said, "You did not stop at the stop sign."

I had not stopped at the stop sign. I thought to myself that I wouldn't be able to get my license. He asked me if I had a car. I said no, but that I would go buy a car if I got my license. I told him that I had two kids at home. The man gave me my license and said, "Drive carefully."

When I got my license, my husband said to me, "How did you get your license?"

He was so jealous. He did not want me to have a car.

I had my license for a while, but I didn't get a car because I was still afraid to drive. My girlfriend told me that I needed to drive so that I could work outside and get my freedom. I asked her if she wanted to go with me to buy a car.

As soon as I had my car, I went to night school. I learned how to read and write, but I was so busy that I couldn't concentrate. I had no time to study.

I took skin care classes at an exclusive Manhattan salon. It was 5 years before I got my diploma for international skin care there. After I finished that, I studied electrolysis. That took several more years. I took the train into New York City for all these classes.

After I finished that, I took make-up classes. When I graduated, I worked with a salon in Westport, Connecticut, as an expert in skin care. I moved to Westport about this time and lived there for awhile.

After about five years living in Westport, I went to Florida for a little vacation. I drove there my by myself. I stayed at my girlfriend's condominium for about a month and had a nice time there. The cold weather had been getting to me and I thought I needed a change. The weather in Connecticut was so different than in Tai Pai, where the temperature was about 50 degrees during the coldest part of the year, and we never had snow. It rained a lot there, though.

On the drive back from Florida I got lost the first night. At a rest stop I asked an older, safe looking man for directions. He told me that there was no one around who would be able to tell me.

Then I heard a car go by. It was going very fast. I drove and tried to catch up with it, but it was going too fast. Then I stopped again and went to sleep at a gas station. Finally I followed a car with a Connecticut license plate and it took me all the way up to New York. I did not even know that I had gotten to New York.

I drove back to Connecticut, but. I did not know the roads. I followed a map that had Connecticut on it, but I was so scared. After that, I didn't travel too far from home anymore.

Then I went to live at my girlfriend's house in White Plains for a while. I lived with her for a month while I looked for a new job.

One day I decided to go and visit the town of Greenwich. I remember parking my car because the streets are so pedestrian friendly there. I decided to amble around and peek in the windows of the shops along the way. It seemed so peaceful and friendly. I loved the long rows of shops.

I fell in love with the main street there, called Greenwich Avenue, which is a mile long. The street was quiet at that time. Now, it is crowded. There are lots of Mercedes Benz. There are lots of condominiums. There are lots of tall buildings. Many New Yorkers have come to Greenwich to raise their children, and they have a lot of activities for children here now. There is still a little bit of country left in Greenwich, though, if you go outside of town. Greenwich has some beautiful homes.

I got two different jobs. One was working for a lady in Greenwich as a companion. The other job was working for Sheer Artistry Salon in Greenwich on Greenwich Avenue. I just walked in there and got a job. I was doing facials. Eddie Santos and Mario owned the business and Eddie, who was the boss, originally hired me.

In the daytime, I worked there at the beauty salon. In the evening, I worked as a companion.

The lady I worked for was irritable. It was a difficult job because she did not respect me and was terrible to me. She would yell at me. I was miserable.

I started knitting sweaters because it helped me mentally. I would go to the library every Sunday to read my books and magazines. I was off that day. In those days I stayed to myself and went quietly about my business.

When I gave the woman notice, she asked me to stay. I told her I just couldn't. I got paid fairly well, but I needed to do something else. I wanted to work at my profession. I had trained so hard in school and had invested a lot of time. I had saved enough money so I could get my own apartment and pay for the security. This was twenty-five years ago.

I looked for an apartment and luckily found a nice studio located across from the Hyatt Regency in Old Greenwich. The hotel was still being built at that time. I lived there for about four years.

I had a single bed, a couch, and a wok. Mostly I ate steamed rice. I was happy there. In the daytime, it was noisy because of the construction that was under way at the Hyatt. As I settled in to my new apartment, I gradually began acquiring some new possessions.

I enjoyed my job at Sheer Artistry. I was new in town and I didn't know anybody, but they were nice to me there. Sometimes Eddie and Mario would take me out to lunch. They were both decent bosses.

The salon was one of several large salons in town. There were probably about twenty people, mostly girls, working there. I was doing skin care, facials and make-up artistry. When no one was there, we would amuse ourselves, kid around and laugh a lot. The day passed by quickly because it was fun. I was very happy, and I made a lot of friends there. Working there helped me forget my problems.

Eddie and I still work together on Greenwich Avenue and we are still good friends.

Eventually, I left Sheer Artistry and I went to work for Carlo and Company. The business belonged to a husband and wife team, Carlo and Mary Lou. This salon was also one of the larger salons in Greenwich. Carlo and Mary Lou were nice to me, too, and I was so appreciative of how they treated me because I still didn't know many people there. They made me feel as if I was part of their family. They are still my friends to this day.

After Carlo and Co., I decided to open a small business of my own. I had worked many years to save my money and I opened Shun Mie's Skin Clinic. It was on Putnam Avenue in Old Greenwich. I had seven girls working for me. Before I opened up, I remodeled the place.

I was busy and I worked very hard, but I didn't have a paycheck because I was paying all the other girls. I had to come up with their paychecks every week. In addition, I had to spend money on rent, liability insurance, electricity, employee compensation, phones, business taxes, equipment for the store, building insurance, advertisements, repayment of loans (plus interest), and cleaning services. The bills rolled in non-stop.

Sometimes I didn't have enough to cover my expenses and eventually I had to eliminate four of the girls.

Still, it was not great. I worked very hard, but at that time, the economy was not good at all. It was 1987 and the stock market had just crashed. All business was bad. I downsized again.

If I had it to do over, there are a few things that I would change. First, I would have bought a small business book to study. Second, I would not have remodeled the building that I leased. I wouldn't recommend remodeling a business unless you have a lot of capital. Additionally, when you are alone, it is very difficult because you don't have anybody there to back you up. It's not easy to save money, but spending money is very easy. When you are alone, you must be very careful as to what you do with your money. Don't think you are going to get the money back because you aren't. Third, you have to have a lot of capital. I didn't have it.

If you want to open a small business, you must do your homework. Your employees will not work as hard as you do, either, and you have to realize that.

I moved my office to Greenwich Avenue where Outdoor Traders used to be. I went very small and I only had a few employees working for me. I stayed there for a couple of years.

Finally I left there because I had decided I wanted to work alone, and that place was too big for me. I didn't want to have employees so I went to a very small office by myself. It was great.

When I had employees, I could never go to lunch. It was too hectic with too long hours. I was exhausted. Sometimes, if employees were sick, I had to do everybody's work.

The only way I work now is by appointment. When I don't have work at the office, I do things outside for myself. I take my lunch when I want to. I take a walk in the fresh air if I want to. Now, I can relax. If I don't have any clients, I can even go home to relax.

When you get a little older, you learn how to rest and to take care of yourself. I even have gained a little weight. I used to weigh about 95 pounds, but now I weigh about 120 pounds. Sometimes when a person worries and gets depressed, they can gain weight. That's because their stomach is not digesting properly. Their thyroid may not be working properly, either. Other people might lose weight, though.

One of my specialties in business is treating skin problems. One time a gentleman called me and told me he had a daughter who was seventeen and had acne. He asked me if I would treat it, and I said yes.

He brought her in for a consultation. I took a look at her and told him it would take me about three months to correct it. Her face was swollen. She was also depressed. She had told him that if her skin did not get better, she was going to kill herself. The more stressed out you are, the more your face will break out, all the more so if you are a teenager going through puberty. Very few teenagers have clear skin.

Her father had heard about a place in France that had a special skin care unit. He told me that before he took her there, he had decided to see me.

On her first appointment I cleaned all of the impurities out of her skin through a deep pore cleansing facial. I gave her a special diet, as well, to be followed stringently. Sometimes what you eat causes problem skin. She had been taking a lot of medication and it had aggravated her skin problems.

Her skin was fair again after the three months.

I used to have bad allergies. I was allergic to everything. The doctor recommended that I should get a shot once a week, so I did. I went to get a shot one day about 11:00 in the morning and afterward I went to my office. Two hours later I was sitting at my desk and my two fingers started to get numb. I had never experienced anything like this before. Then my whole body went numb.

My office was two minutes from Greenwich Hospital so I went to the emergency room. They just let me lie there until a doctor came and checked me out. I stayed there for another two hours. I had asked them to call my doctor, but they never did. I don't think they felt my condition was very serious because they didn't give me anything to take. About four hours later, they sent me home.

The next day, I started to have stomach pain. It felt like someone had stabbed me. I went to the doctor in my apartment building. He gave me something to take, but nothing changed. My stomach was still in a lot of pain. I got very sick then and I went to another doctor, who gave me something else to take.

Two weeks later, I was not any better.

I started to have heart palpitations. I called an ambulance and went to Stamford Hospital. I wouldn't go to Greenwich Hospital again. Stamford Hospital sent me home. By this time, I had probably been to five different doctors.

I could not eat. In a month, I had lost 28 pounds.

My girlfriend came to visit me and the same day took me to Milford Hospital.

That doctor would not let me go home. He admitted me into the hospital and I was there for one week. I got a little better. The color in my face improved, but I still did not feel right. After the week was up, they released me, but I was not completely better.

When I got back home, I started to meditate twice a day. I still felt sick from the hospital, too, and all I could eat was rice and some vegetables. There was not enough nutrition in them for me, though, because I was still so weak.

I went back to my own doctor and I told him how weak I was and that I had no energy. He gave me something to take, but I still did not feel right.

One day I went to lunch with a friend. I couldn't touch my food and I ate nothing.

The woman sitting next to me asked me what was wrong and I told her all that had happened to me. She told me she wanted to take me to a Chinese doctor in Chinatown. She insisted I go. She even made the appointment for me and took me there.

The doctor talked to me for awhile and then he worked on me for an hour. Before I left his office, I was very tired and I fell asleep in the car on the way home.

When I got home, I boiled the herbs he had given me for about a half hour before I drank them. Afterward I felt like something happened to my system and I felt really good.

I took the herbs twice a day. He had given me a thirty day supply, but after I had taken them for a few days, I felt increasingly better each time.

A week later, I could eat food. My stomach got better. I felt as if I had rejuvenated myself.

Because I had been so weak, someone came to my house and gave me a massage once a week. I also massaged my own stomach and did reflexology. I took the herbs for about two months altogether.

In a month or two, I was back to myself again. My allergies had gone away, too.

After all this, I really watched what I ate. I rested a lot. I gained my weight back. That was ten years ago and after that, my allergies have never bothered me. Before that I had been allergic to everything in the air. When I went out, I would have to cover up my head.

I had gotten allergies because I didn't get enough sleep and I didn't eat right. I never ate three meals a day. I was worried a lot and I didn't have any appetite. I used to take medications sometimes and I had to get shots once a week for about five years. I wasn't sleeping well. I was drinking a lot of coffee everyday. I had no time whatsoever. I never watched television then because I didn't have time.

I was so busy that sometimes I didn't know what day it was. One time it was a Sunday and I just got up and went to work. Afterward, on Sundays, I put my living room curtain up so I would remember not to go to work.

When I was in Milford Hospital I had told myself that I had to survive and had to stop killing myself.

Since then I eat three meals a day. I take five vitamins. I rest. I don't take any more pills or any shots. My diet is steamed vegetables. I don't drink coffee. I drink decaffeinated tea. I don't eat any fried foods or any dairy. I eat all kinds of fruits.

It is important for me to gargle my throat with warm salt water every night. If I want to use candles, I use lemon scented candles. If you have a dog or cat, by the way, don't let them in your room. Your bedroom must be dust-free.

I recommend just living day by day. I was sick with allergies for ten years, but I haven't had allergies for the last ten years now.

It has been over thirty years now since I emigrated from Taiwan to the United States.

After I arrived here with my husband and my little girl in 1968, it became an ongoing struggle for our small family. The culture here was so incredibly foreign to me that I felt a lost. After having come from a small rural village with a small population, I was not only intimidated by the fast paced environment here, I was overwhelmed.

I had to learn so much in such a short time just to keep up with everyone else. Fortunately when I got here, I spoke the little bit of English which I had learned when I used to keep company with a missionary's daughter who spoke fluent English.

Every time I went through a great deal of tragedy, I always remembered what my father told me: "Your mind has a lot to do with everything you do in your life. Whatever you put in your mind, you can go with. When you are sick, it is a big deal. Never put the thought into your head that that's it. Put into your head that you are going to make it. It's very important in life what you have upstairs there."

Every time something bad happened to me, I remembered what my father said. The last time I had an allergic reaction, I lost so much weight that I was not myself. Then I said to myself that I could do it. All I did was to meditate and pray. I talked to myself, but I didn't talk to anyone else. I disciplined myself.

Sometimes when I went through a tragedy, I thought in my mind of everything my father had taught me. I think he was my guardian angel. When he was around, he would always tell me a story and now I always have these stories in my mind when something goes wrong.

This has worked for me. It has helped to make me strong. My father always said, "Life is strange sometimes. Life is up and down. Life is not smooth."

Once he was talking to me about the Bible and he said, "The Bible said the temperature is never the same. It gets cold. It gets hot. It gets warm. Life is the same thing. Every day, every year, we feel differently inside us. It is best to think that you should not feel weak. Strong, meaning strong in your head, is very, very important."

That was the best thing my father taught me growing up: be strong, don't worry, take care of yourself. He also said that no one else knows how you feel.

When I get sick, I always think of him, and I hear him talking to me in my ear. "When you get sick, don't ever say to yourself, 'I'm not going to make it.'"

Think positively. Don't panic. Try not to be depressed. Even if a doctor tells you that you have a few months to live, don't absorb this as true. Don't think that way. Never accept it.

You have to tell yourself, "I'm going to make it."

We're too soft. Some people would fall for that negative diagnosis, but survival takes a lot of courage and strength. Every time I pray, I ask for courage and strength. Sometimes I think God tests us to see how much we can take while we live in this world. We go through so many things in this life, up and down.

When you go through all of these struggles, though, I think that it makes you stronger.

CHAPTER III
<u>RELATIONSHIPS WITH MEN</u>

<u>Older Women Dating Younger Men</u>

Some women might feel awkward or strange going out with a younger man. There are couples who get married with this age difference and are happy, but it is somewhat unusual.

There are advantages to being with a younger man. Young men are very energetic, so these men can generally keep up with you. Most of the time, they are fun to be with. They can be happy. They laugh. And that's what some women need.

While it's okay for an older woman to date a younger man, she may have ongoing fears and worries because of the age difference. The older woman may also have grown children, yet he may not have ever been married. If the relationship goes beyond dating and begins to get serious, the woman has to think seriously about what to do. She has to think about the consequences for herself and for him, too. There are far reaching consequences that the two of them might not even be aware of at first, and these can affect them later on.

One woman was seeing a man who was much younger than she was. She looked at him and she knew she could fall in love with him very fast. That was her initial feeling. At first, when they just went out, it wasn't romantic. They were basically friends because she was too afraid to get involved. She tried to prevent herself from getting hurt, but she was disappointed because she liked this man. She wondered to herself why she met this man at this time because she felt if she had met him earlier in her life, things could have been different.

She did not see him for a while. She did not know it until later, but he had gotten married and had children.

From time to time she would see him by accident because they lived in the same town. Sometimes he would call her on the telephone to see how she was doing. He would stop at her office once in a while, too.

Now she didn't want to see him. Then he called her and told her he had become separated. She still did not want to see him. She felt his life was too complicated and besides, she felt funny because he wasn't divorced yet and he had two children. She felt that he could reconcile with the wife at any time. She didn't think going out with him was the right thing to do.

More than six years went by. Occasionally he would still stop by her office to see her. He had not gotten her out of his system, even after all those years. Sometimes she would feel more warmly toward him and she would feel herself weakening.

Then, for a long time, he did not call or stop by to see her. She was kind of happy, yet she became confused again when she saw him again. He had stopped by her work place unexpectedly.

After he left the office, she was very upset. Half of her thought she should call him and tell him she wanted to get together; the other half of her put up a stone wall.

Sometimes he would call her and his voice sounded sexy. If only he was the same age, she thought, she could marry him and live happily ever after.

Again she did not see him or hear from him for a couple of years. When she would think of him, she became sad. Tears would well up in her eyes and run down her cheeks. She was relieved on one hand; on the other, she was distraught.

From time to time, she had dreams about him. In them he was with her romantically. Even though she did not see him and they did not get together, she thought about him constantly.

Sometimes she would picture him in her mind and then he would call her or she would accidentally see him. She was confused for many years. She would not date anyone because she felt like she was still waiting for him.

They had some kind of special, strong chemistry even though they had never slept together.

One day, when she had not seen him for a couple of years, she came into her office and found a message waiting for her on her machine. It was his voice again. He had said, "I didn't see you for a very long time. I wanted to know how you are doing." She thought it was a nice message and she grew excited.

She called him back. He asked her if she wanted to get together with him just for dinner. She was excited to be able see him again, and he was excited to see her.

They met for dinner together at a nice restaurant, and he told her that he had gotten a divorce. She wasn't sure whether to believe him, but she still had such warm feelings toward him.

She wanted to meet his children, but he never asked her to. Then one day, quite by accident, she saw him in the distance down the street and when he came up to her, his children were with him. They were smart and cute. They talked to her. Then, another time, she saw him again with his children and there was a brief exchange between them all.

The next day after their dinner date, she went for a walk to the park. She stopped at a picnic table. The sky was clear blue, but the weather was getting cold. She felt a little lonely inside. She lay down on the grass and looked up. The sky looked so pretty to her and she thought of him and how much she wanted to be close to him.

She had always held herself back with him, but now she started to talk to herself and to wonder why she had put herself in that situation. She had first become involved with him when he had not been married and did not have children. Then he got married and had children. Now, even though he got a divorce, she could not bring herself to break off their relationship.

Sometimes, when you are in love with someone, even though you don't see him, you can still have strong feelings for him which are difficult to explain. When you see the person, you get all warm, and you forget what you are supposed to say. Your brain shuts down because you are so attracted to the person. In front of them you can't think straight. You melt like sugar.

This woman remained confused. Sometimes she felt like she didn't want to see him or to talk to him ever again.

After a while he called her and begged to see her. She couldn't resist. They went out to dinner. They talked. He told her that he spent a lot of time with his children. She thought that he really did not have time or energy for her in his life because his two children were so young and active.

Her feelings did not change towards him, but she decided not to go near him again because it could was too complicated for her. Later that evening they went to a movie, but at the end of the evening, they went their separate ways. He said he would call her the next day and he did.

For all of those years, she had feelings for this man and she thought she was in love with him. She was left to wonder what the man really felt toward her because he never told her how he felt. She wanted to know, but to this day, she is still unsure about his feelings for her. Sometimes this bothers her because she still has such strong feelings for him, yet she is forced to live with the uncertainty. It plagues her.

They continued to communicate and see each other, but they were not really together. In her mind, though, they were together even if it remains a wish or sort of a fantasy.

She never called him. She told herself that if she ever called him, she would break her own fingers for dialing. Instead, she waited for him to call.

When he called, he said to her, "I didn't hear from you. I thought you were going to call me."

She told him, "I thought you were going to call me. We have poor communication."

They argued about it a little bit.

He told her, "I left you a message that you should call me if you have time. I was waiting for you. I was so patient waiting for your call."

She remained confused and continued to think about their relationship.

The next time she saw him, she told him she had had dream about him. She dreamed that she saw a girl with blonde curly hair with him.

She had thought that he really was with another girl and so thought that she should not take him so seriously. The dream, she felt, told her that there was someone else there with him besides her.

The next time they saw each other on the street, he had said to her, "I miss you."

She said, "I miss you, too."

He asked her to get together for dinner to celebrate his birthday, but she had the wrong day and they did not see each other.

Because of the dream she had had about seeing him with the blonde haired girl, she had come to think that he had been avoiding him. She felt like he had someone else there for himself. That told her she had better cool the whole thing off.

He became angry and upset with her.

To this day their story goes on and on...

Another woman went on vacation to her girlfriend's house in Long Island. She met a man there who was visiting her girlfriend at the same time. They started talking together.

He had a job in Maine, but he was from Long Island. They started getting to know one another. He liked to go fishing so she went along with him. They seemed to speak the same language, and they got along well together, but he did not know how old she was.

When she went back home to New York, he went home to Maine. They kept communicating and she invited him to come to New York on his next vacation.

They spent a week together at her house, and again they got along very well. Then they went on a fishing vacation together to Nantucket. They got together again two weeks later on Long Island.

A month later, they were together again in Kennebunkport. They rented a cottage with a kitchenette for a week and they fished together every day. He would catch the fish and she would cook them.

She would go for a walk every day. She was happy. He was enjoying himself, too.

Then one day, she said to herself, "This is getting too close, too deep." She was so much older than he was. She thought of telling him, but didn't. Each time after they had been together, on a vacation or even on a date, she would miss him very much.

They called each other twice a day.

After two weeks of being apart after Kennebunkport, he went to stay with his mother. He called his girlfriend and asked her to meet him in Long Island. He was bringing her to meet his mother.

After they had all visited, his mother did not say anything to him.

The girlfriend felt like the mother liked her, but she was not sure. She began to worry that she would get hurt. She had gotten too involved, she thought, and she started feeling sad. She felt that she had been through a lot because she had been married once and had two children whom she had raised alone. The man had never been married.

He asked her to go to Puerto Vallarta, Mexico, and they stayed in that town two weeks.

When they went out dancing at night, they stayed up late. She went out too with a husband and wife that she met there. Then he would go out by himself and later she would meet him in the places where he liked to go hang out.

One night she was sitting in a night spot with him and she became friendly with the man who was sitting next to her. She asked him if she could tell him his fortune. He agreed.

She told him that he had not seen his mother for a long time. She also told him that since he was the only grown up son his mother had, his mother was very sad. She wanted to talk to him. After she had told him the rest of his fortune, the man went to call his mother.

When he came back to the table, he told her that his mother was so happy to hear from him and that she was crying so much they could not really talk. He told her that he would call her back that night.

She went back the next day to the same place. He was there again. He asked her how she knew all of this and he said he would visit his mother often from then on. She asked him to promise to do this and he said, "Okay."

She started swimming classes where she danced in the water to the music.

She would get up very early in the morning and walk on the beach. Every time she walked there by herself, she would see a man sitting in one spot on the beach.

One day the man came up to her and they started talking. The man asked her if she came there alone, and she said no, that she had come there with a friend, but she didn't say whether she had come there with a male or a female friend.

Every morning, he was waiting there for her. One day they went for a walk together. Then he followed her to the hotel where she was staying. She told him that she was going to go to breakfast. He asked her if he could go with her and she said, "Okay."

He had started to like her. He told her that he was married, but that his wife did not like to get up early. After breakfast he asked her what she was doing that day, but. she already had made plans to go with the married couple to see a place where Elizabeth Taylor once made a movie.

The same night she went with her boyfriend to a restaurant where they danced with each other exclusively. Her boyfriend was an exceptionally good dancer, and she loved to dance too.

That night something got to her. She became completely touched with him and was warmed all over by him. It was very special, but she felt that this could not be forever. She thought she was too old for him, and this bothered her terribly. She could no longer have children, but he said that he did not care and that he still wanted to be with her.

She started to tell him that they should slow down. She wanted him to get married to someone else and have a family while he was young. He said he did not care, and that he really wanted to be with her. He told her that he loved her and that he wanted to be with her. His parents did not object and they didn't interfere. He had told his mother that he wanted to live with her and told his mother that he loved her.

After that vacation, even though they had been going out for two and a half years, they did not see each other for a while because she had gotten so scared. She felt she was too attached to him and too involved.

They would still talk regularly. He would call her every other day. She told him that she had mixed feelings. Even so, he asked her to go on vacation to California. She said no and did not go. All she knew was that she wanted him to get married and have a family.

About a month later they did go on vacation to Long Island. She kept telling him that he should find someone else and have a family. He did not like that. She told him to have children while he was young. She was serious. She knew she was much older than he was, and as much as she loved him, she wanted what she felt was best for him, and for her too.

A month or two later, he was still calling her and wanting to get together. He kept telling her how much he missed her and how much he wanted for them to be together. She always said no.

One day he called her and told her he wanted to get together. Every time he called her she would soften just listening to his voice. She still wanted him to go on with his life, though. She felt that their relationship should not continue because of their age difference and that she would not be comfortable spending her life with him.

This kept nagging at her, but he kept calling her in spite of it.

Finally she said to him, "Do you think this is easy for me? Half of me wants to be with you and the other half wants you to have the life you deserve with a wife your own age and children."

She told him, "Let's end it. If you really care for me, you have to stay away from me."

Then she said, "As long as I live, I will never forget you."

She was sad for a long time after this. Sometimes she wished that she never had met him.

For two years, she heard nothing from him. Then she heard from her girlfriend that he had gotten married and had had children. After two years of being married, the marriage went on the rocks. She felt sorry for him. He called her. He told her he just wanted to talk. She talked to him, and he told her he wanted to see her. She told him that he was married now and had children and he should try to make that work.

One day he called her and told her that he had gotten a divorce. He had come to New York to see her. She was dating someone else, but they went out to dinner and she told him that she had been dating a man for a while. She told him that she just wanted to date one man at a time because she did not want to confuse her feelings. She told him that it was probably better not to get back together because it would confuse her. Now she was dating a nice guy and she would not want to hurt his feelings.

After that, they never heard from each other again. He kept calling her, but she would not answer the phone. Finally she had to change her phone number.

That was the end.

He was still in love with her and she was still in love with him. She never really had gotten over this man. She would always think of him. For a long time she even felt that he was still with her. She had to talk to herself and tell herself, "Try to forget him." The feelings stayed with her for a long time.

Sometimes women who are very sensitive have special feelings for men, and it is difficult to forget those men. To help forget, they should work with charities helping people and with children who need help.

When an older woman is dating a younger man, although it has become more popular in our society today, it is not an easy thing. There are issues that are bound to come up. That couple has to deal with things they might not see at first. It can be very complicated later on, as it was in the stories above.

In the beginning stages of the relationship, it may be a chic thing to do or fun, but later on you will start to worry when he is out late. You will not feel good. You will always be worried. You are going to be a nervous wreck. It won't be healthy.

At first, you might think you will be able to handle the stress, but it will likely take a toll on you, both physically and psychologically.

The first woman kept holding back with her man because she was older than he was, and he did not want to sleep with her unless they were married. They would go out to dinner and go to the movies. Sometimes they would stay at home and watch television and hold hands. Other evenings they would do things independent of each other and still feel secure within their relationship. They felt that a relationship would last longer this way.

He always told her that he wanted to give her an engagement ring, but she said she didn't want one. She didn't want to commit to him and she held back because of their age difference. Not only that, but she felt he was comfortable by himself. She felt living together could be dangerous to their relationship because he had never lived with anyone before. They saw each other all of the time, so he thought that maybe they should live together.

Another couple, she older, he younger, had known each other for many years, but did not feel any necessity to consummate their relationship. They really loved each other and they loved each other's company. They were secure. They trusted one another. They knew that each of them was not going to go anywhere else. Their relationship was solid.

They told each other everything that was going on with each of them. They weren't nervous like other people who can often pressure the people they are with. They liked to keep their relationship this way. They both felt good with each other. They never talked about money. They were happy this way. It worked for them.

Looking for a Husband

When you are looking for a husband, you must not act as if you are a big spender. Act like you like to cook and take care of the house. Talk about your job. Act like a serious person. Keep your conversations light at first. Every time you say something, think before you open your mouth.

If you really like a man, don't take him home for a long time. Don't ask him to go to expensive restaurants. Let him ask you. Go to his house first so you know how he lives. Some men are very neat.

Don't try to kiss him for a while. He'll respect you. Otherwise, he will think you do that with everybody.

Don't wear heels that are too high because he will think you are cheap. Also, watch what he wears. If he wears jeans a lot, you can wear jeans too. If he does not know how to dress himself, and if you really like him, take him shopping and dress him up.

Never pay for a dinner, even if you have a lot of money.

Never talk about sex. Let him talk about it. Read a man's face and his body language—this is very important. Physical contact is one of the most important contributions to a feeling of inner warmth. Feeling and touching are so important. Everyone who cares about another deeply needs physical contact, and touching each other in romantic ways can be such gratifying physical contact.

For a woman to feel a man is really interested in her, he must buy her flowers once in a while. He should send them to her house or to where she works. Even a single rose or an orchid can be symbolic of his feelings for her.

Don't call a man too much. Let him call you. If he calls you, return the call. Don't initiate the calls, though, because he will think you are desperate and are just chasing him. If you have known him for a long time, you can call him two or three times a day, but you have to have known him for a long time.

If you really care for a man, start "training" him to be the way you want him to be. See if he is responsive. Have him do simple things—pick up groceries, milk, and so forth. Let that man do things. It's good. If he doesn't do it, then you have to let him go. Today the woman shouldn't have to do everything.

Today there are some men who will easily tell you they "love you" with a specific motive in mind. Generally, when it comes to relationships, women are warm toward men, whereas these men are cold. Even though they might think they want you in their life, when you start the relationship, they can change their minds fast. Sometimes you have already become warm with him, yet you feel lonely. You are with these men and you have the physical contact, but you have no real connection.

These men cannot do too may different things. Because they are not as strong as a woman is, they talk sweet, but inside they are sour, like lemon juice. They are only sweet when they kiss you and hold you tight. You think they are ready to care for you, but they do that because they want sex. After they get sex, they become cold and have no emotions whatsoever.

These men can take a lot of energy from you.

Some other men are always looking for someone else better than the woman they're going out with. They are not really vested in you. Once they think they have you, they already start moving on to someone else who in their minds is better.

Women show more affection than these men do. When women start to get warm, these men can shy away because they have "unfinished business" out there. They can be afraid, too. In either case, these men can just leave you hanging. They will often be in a relationship with one foot in and one foot out.

A woman should move on and not wait for a man unless the man has shown a vested interest.

Never show a man you are desperate.

If you don't see anything happening with a man, move on fast. In no time at all, a woman can end up saying to herself, "What happened to me that I'm forty already?" Not every man cares what happens to you.

Some men like to play games. They don't take women seriously because they think they are better than we are, especially if they have money.

You can tell when a man really likes you by the way he acts. If a man doesn't make decisions on his own, without you, he really cares for you. A man won't go away without you, either, if he really loves you. He'll want to spend money on you.

Remember it is never too late for a man to have a relationship if he has money. He can be ninety years old.

A woman can't do that. It is not the same for us. The world, unfortunately, is really like this.

The Woman Who Has Everything, Except a Man

You say you have everything.

But if you are lonely, there is a void in your life. Maybe you don't want somebody to come into your life. You might be afraid because of something that happened to you in the past. Maybe you have a fear that you will be let down again. Through all this time you are so sad that it holds you back. It shows on your face.

In this world, you cannot have everything. But you can still try to achieve the most happiness that life can afford you.

Find happiness in the simple things, in the beauty of a flower, in listening to the rain. Learn to appreciate the natural beauty that abounds on the earth. It is everywhere. Go to museums. Get interested in art. Find happiness.

Then someone will find you.

When you do go out, don't act like you have everything. If you wear expensive clothing and jewelry, the man might be intimidated. It depends on what you are looking for. Do you want to be serious or are do you just want to have fun?

Don't look too hard.

Sometimes you may try to look for someone in a singles group. Going to single events is only good once in a while. If you do it on a regular basis, you see the same people there. It is difficult because even if you are there, it is a little desperate. It is a forced, contrived situation. Unless you are at a special event, you might feel as if you are in a lonely hearts club. It is embarrassing.

This has happened to me.

First Date

What do you do the first time you meet a man?

This first time you meet a man, you must shake his hand. If when you take his hand, he grabs your hand with strength, this man is trying to impress you. This man is strong mentally and physically. If you marry this man he will be a good provider. He is strong inside and out.

With a weak grip, a man wants you to take care of him. With a soft handshake, a man is not very intuitive in what he does. He is on the lazy side (this is true, man or woman). He is slow at everything he does.

Look at his palm color and if it is yellow or has no color, the man drinks too much or smokes a lot. Light pale means he has bad circulation. The palm of a strong person has a reddish color (man or woman). A red palm shows a very aggressive person (man or woman). Pale palmed people are not clever. Pink and red palms are normal; they show vitality and activity.

It is very important how you present yourself—especially on a first date. You want to be attractive and alluring, but you don't want to be too sexy. If you look too sexy, he might get the wrong signals and think you are mostly interested in a sexual relationship.

Even if you normally drink a lot, just have one or two drinks at the most with him. When you order dinner, if you order too much food, you could scare him off because he will think you are high maintenance. It is very important to listen first to what he says. If he asks you questions, answer him, but don't volunteer. Don't ask him too many questions, though.

Sometimes the less you say, the better.

Relax. Have a good time.

When a man talks, you should remember what he says because if you don't, he's going to think you are just looking for a warm body that will pick up the bill at the end of the evening.

If you care, you have to listen. If you don't care about him, don't date him.

The next time you see him, compare what he says to the last time you saw him. Some men could be bluffing.

It's very important not to talk about money. If you have a lot of money, don't tell him. He can talk about money, but not you.

You should know what he does.

If a man tells you how much money he has in the bank, watch out. If he does that, he's probably trying too hard to impress you. There must be an underlying reason.

On the first date, don't go home with a man and don't take him home. I don't care how desperate you are. If he's handsome and sexy, maybe you want to, but don't do it. Take your time. Cool off.

Some men may test you and try your willpower to see what kind of woman you are. They will sometimes deliberately make you jealous so that you think you are lucky if you get them. They do it to speed the relationship up. They try to get you excited by thinking every woman is hot for them. They test you.

Watch out for this because, although they are not necessarily playing you, they are not ready to commit and they want to keep control of you so you don't go with another man. Even though they are not sure if they want you, they might want to keep looking themselves. These men might not have too much to offer. This all could be a smoke screen.

If a man talks about his girlfriends or his wife, you have to slow down with him. If he just went through a break-up or divorce, he'll need a lot of time. Take it slowly.

It's very important to act like a lady. Don't talk too much. Later on you can, but not at first.

If you don't know a man too well, you must find out where he works or lives.

If you don't like a man on a first date, tell him that you have five kids at home. Tell him you have to go home by 10:00 or 11:00 p.m. because the babysitter is waiting for you. This is rather extreme, but sometimes you might have to resort to this if he is really after you.

However, the best way to exit is to say that you are busy and you have to get up early for work.

If something is bothering you or if you have something going on, never discuss it. If you do bring it up, a man is not likely to talk about it again. Talk about something funny or something philosophical or something intelligent.

Don't show too much emotion. Don't act desperate. If you don't see a man again, it's not the end of the world.

Don't get attached to a man until he spends a significant amount of money on you That means he has "invested" in you and in having a relationship with you.

If a man asks you to go out on the weekend, that means he really likes you, or it could mean he wants to be seen with you in public, or it could just mean he has nothing better to do. He might be killing time until something better comes along. Don't be fooled by this man's sweet talk.

Most men will engage in sweet talk. There are very few men who will talk to you straight up and not lead you on. These men who do talk straight to you are, unfortunately, the exception. It is a sad reality of the heterosexual culture within our society in the western world. You're not going to change it, so you just have to smile, be as happy as you can, and adapt to it by graciously accepting it.

Don't show a man everything at once. If you do, then there's nothing left for him to find out.

Never wear silver when you go out on a date because, whatever you wear, that's what he'll buy you.

The first time you look at a man, he might look like he is a nobody. You have to study him. He could be a very important person. He might not know how to dress, or he might not want to dress to impress people in a certain way. You have to get to know him.

Never talk too much about yourself. Let him talk. You have to find out what his background is. He could be the nicest guy you ever met.

You have to make a man like you first. See him many times. Never ask him outright where he works. Never ask him about his car.

If a man is too well manicured and too meticulously dressed, be careful. You'll have to really get to know this man. He might just be out to impress you and then later dump you for no reason.

Being a Model

Once there was a woman who was a model.

When someone is a model, she represents what our society decides is a picture of what a woman is supposed to be to be beautiful. It is a high pressure career. A model has a beautiful figure, a beautiful face and is poised. She often makes a lot of money.

This particular model was surrounded by a lot of people. Sometimes she could barely breathe. She had a lot of trouble sleeping. She was invited to many social events, and life for her was just one party after another. People liked to have her around because she was beautiful.

She became mentally and physically exhausted.

When a woman is a model, she sometimes can think life is always going to be like that.

This woman thought her looks were never going to change. She could not realize that when she got older; things were bound to change for her. She didn't take life too seriously.

She did not realize that you couldn't party all of the time. If you do, it will take its toll on you. When a model dates men, the relationships don't last too long. Many men dated her, but the men didn't hang around too long because she was very high maintenance.

In this atmosphere, there was a strong temptation for her to get involved with drugs and alcohol. This woman started partying too much. She began to age prematurely. She stayed up too late and she didn't get enough rest. It was a life of extremes.

She started looking older and she started gaining weight. Slowly, everything started to change for her. People started not to take her seriously.

She began to fall apart.

At one point she got married and had a son, but she never took care of her son. The nanny had to do take care of him all the time and the child began to think that the nanny was his mother.

She was not prepared for the future. She did not save money or plan ahead. Her husband divorced her when her child was still young. Her life went downhill from there on. Later on, she could hardly pay the rent.

The last time I saw her she was really down.

I told her, "Right now, it's not you talking. It's the drugs and liquor."

She picked on me and told me my English was bad.

So I said, "I'm not your friend anymore. I don't like to hang around anyone who takes drugs and drinks so heavily."

That was it. This woman was very selfish. She didn't realize that her friends would dump her. She thought her friends couldn't live without her and that she would always be the center of attention. She could not believe that she wound up with no friends.

She tried to get a job, but she was too washed up and acted too flaky. She would make appointments for interviews and show up looking awful. When she finally was able to get a job, she would not show up.

The last time I saw her, she told me she was moving to California.

Dating on the Internet

Many people now write to each other on the Internet.

It's advisable that you get a sample of handwriting from a man you meet on the Internet before you go out with him.

If you meet a man on the Internet, talk to him on the telephone before you meet him and listen carefully to his voice.

If he talks too slow, he has no action. He thinks you are going to do all the work for him, make all the arrangements and so forth. If his voice is too soft, then this is not good, physically or mentally. If the person talks too fast, all he'll want to do is talk your head off.

Some men talk slowly because they want to listen to you. These are the smartest men. Go for them.

Sometimes, though, when a man talks too slowly, you shouldn't say too much. Listen to him first even though he will want to listen to you. This man can read you physically. He'll be very serious. He won't take jokes well. Listen to him a lot. He may have a lot on his mind, but you can't tell at first.

If a man always talks too slowly, he could just be old in his thinking. Talk to him, too, four or five times before you meet him. Then you can figure out what kind of person he actually is. Sometimes there just might not be anybody home, or sometimes he could be a doctor or a professional man and an important person.

If a man talks very fast, then he will do things very fast. He could mess everything up. He is an impulsive person who can make a lot of mistakes. If he talks too fast, then he's not creative. He's driven by money and power and wants to impress. He does not think when he does things. He just does them. You must talk to him four or five times before you agree to meet him. If he talks too fast, he is not prudent. He will like to make you do things fast. He wants you to think he has a lot going on, but he only wants to make believe he has a lot of things to do. He really does not have much to do at all.

If a man talks too sweetly, he has nothing upstairs and nothing in his pockets.

If a man ask you too many questions, you don't have to answer. He's suspicious, and may not be a very nice person. Talk to him a few times. If he's really interested in you, he should ask you what you like to do and where you like to go. If he takes too long to answer you, then that itself is suspicious.

If a man has a strong voice, you can hear he's strong. He could carry you everywhere. He could make things happen. If a man says he wants to just go to local places, then you both have to be ready to accept that.

You don't always have to take what a man says too seriously, though. Go by what he does for you.

If a man from the Internet wants to meet for coffee, it's okay. Then you can leave easily. Take your time with him, and then you can go to dinner with him on the second date. Really listen to his conversation.

Watch the clothes you wear. It's a challenge. Don't show too much. If you overdo it, he will think you will be too expensive for him.

Wear light make-up and not too much jewelry. Somebody can read you by your clothes and by how you present yourself. Have your nails natural.

When you talk, don't volunteer. Listen to him first. Don't talk about politics on the first date or at all, in fact, in the beginning. Talk about the restaurant you are in and make small talk.

If you want somebody old-fashioned, then see if he pulls out your chair and stands up when you go to the ladies' room. Never ask him what he does. Let him tell you. Otherwise, he will think you are after him for his money.

Be aware that by dating from the Internet, you may find a man who is transferring into town. He could just be looking for someone to take care of him. Or he could be unemployed or retired or trying to start a home somewhere.

Dating Your College Sweetheart

Once there were two people in love.

They had met in college, but they were from different backgrounds. They started off being friends and only later on became girlfriend and boyfriend. They fell in love and two years later they were planning on getting married.

They talked about where they were going to live and work and finally they came to Greenwich, CT. They had graduated at the same time and they both had gotten jobs in New York City.

While they had been dating, he never took her to meet his parents and she didn't take him to meet her parents. They didn't want to complicate their lives.

He had tried to talk with his mother, but had only told her that he might get married after he finished college. Her parents did not want her to marry outside of her race so she never brought him home to meet her parents. She told her boyfriend that they could get married anyway and without the consent of their parents.

They were confused, though, and did not know what to do. Finally they went to have their own wedding in Hawaii. They had a wedding and a honeymoon all at the same time.

They were happy.

A few years went by and the couple had a baby.

The boy's mother was a client of my skin clinic and often came to see me. Every time she came, she complained about her back and her neck hurting. Several years went by, but still she would not see her grandbaby. Her husband communicated with the couple, though, and helped them financially.

One day, without calling her, her son came to visit her with his wife and baby. She threw them out. The son and daughter took the baby to the car and sat there and cried.

Her husband was upset and for a long time after, the he did not talk to his wife. She still wouldn't admit that she had done something wrong.

One day she came in to see me and she was in pain. I asked her, "Do you have anyone to talk to?"

"No, not for many years," she said.

So I said, "I want to talk to you. I have known you for a very long time. You have had all of this pain for many years. Something has been bothering you for a very long time. You are missing something. You are missing being with your son, your daughter-in-law and your grandbaby for all of these years. It's not too late. You should call them and really open up to them and tell them you want to meet."

I did not see her for a long time, and then one day I saw them in a restaurant. They were all there, the whole family. They all looked so happy together.

She came over to me when she saw me.

"Shun Mie, thank you so much," she told me. "You saved my life. My family is so happy now because I listened to what you told me."

Another time there was a girl who dated her college sweetheart for about three or four years. They had grown up in different backgrounds too.

When this couple was in college, they always went places together. They did not worry about anything. They just had a good time and their parents paid for all their trips.

They knew they were going to get married after college even though they didn't know where they were going to live or what they were going to do for their careers yet.

He told his mother that he was going to get married after graduation. The mother was not too happy because the girl was of a different faith. She asked her son how he was going to get married when he had no job, no money, and no furniture.

The mother could not tell her son what to do and expect him to listen. The same thing went for the girl. She wouldn't listen to her mother, either.

They lived together during college. When they graduated, they got married by themselves at the local Justice of the Peace. Just a few friends were in attendance.

They both started working. He got a job working in the daytime and she worked at night. They became very busy, but they did not make a lot of money. Sometimes they could hardly pay their bills because they were struggling so much.

They had no parents to help them out.

Single Women who Want to Date after 50 or 60

You may think you are over the hill when you reach 50—60, but your life is only beginning.

You only think you are old. Don't go saying or thinking that you are over that hill. Whatever you are going to do from now on, you are going to do it as if you were a young woman.

This age is a wonderful age because you have experience in life and experience with people.

You are not alone. Your sex life can still be very active. It depends on the man you are with.

Do whatever makes you feel good. Do your hair, your clothes, and take care of your body. If you are a little heavy, do something for yourself.

It's important how you act and how you walk. When you walk in the street, don't act like you are old. When you walk, put your head and chest up and swing your arms just like you were 25 years old.

Don't ever categorize yourself as being old. There are a lot of men out there looking for experienced women. Some men like that.

If you go out on a date, you'll feel better. When you date, don't talk about problems. If anything is wrong with you, don't talk about it. Just have fun. Don't worry. Enjoy yourself and enjoy each other's company. Remember what it felt like to be on a date as a teenager and the thrill of being together and talking and laughing. Laughter is good for the soul. It transfers your problems into another compartment for a while.

In a city you have many places to go. Don't go to restaurants where there are large crowds. Go to expensive places. Go out to upscale places. If you go to poor places, who are you going to meet? Go to places where executives will go.

When you go out, go to the same places. Go where people will see you and can get to know you. Don't go to different places. Otherwise they will think you are fly-by-night. They will feel more comfortable the more they get to know you.

If you go to one of these places because you want to date somebody who is there, that is good, but sooner or later you could also become a permanent friend to him, not just someone a man hopes to get into bed.

So don't stay home. Just go out.

Older Women Dating Older Men

If you are an older woman or older man, you might think your social or dating life is over, but it's isn't. It is only beginning.

You can always go back to the way you were before. Nobody is old. Not anymore.

If you want to socialize, you can join clubs in your area which are designed for people who are single senior citizens. They have music. You can dance. This is one good way to meet people.

Your local churches will likely sponsor events where you can meet people, too. Sometimes there are organized tours that you can go on with other people for culture and fun. You never know who you are going to meet.

Don't be shy. Don't be afraid to go out. The more you start going out, the more you will enjoy yourself and you won't feel so alone. It's not good to stay cooped up in your house.

Get a lot of exercise and you will get rejuvenated.

Sometimes the person you might be interested in is right under your nose, so keep an open mind. There could be a wonderful, intelligent, and witty person in your own town who is just as lonely as you and looking for companionship.

Dating a Man who is Getting a Divorce

If a man is getting a divorce, he is often very confused. This is especially true if he has children. These men don't like rejection.

They don't know what they are doing. They tend to go out with a lot of women so they don't have to get involved or show their feelings.

If you try to get serious with such a man, he knows. Instead of calling you twice a day, he begins to call you twice a week. Instead of him seeing you two or three times a week, he will probably see you once a week. Don't try to talk to him about having a long term relationship because he will probably run away. Don't talk about the future with him. Just talk about the present. Otherwise, he will think it is getting too heavy and he will run away.

Once there was a woman dating what she thought was and whom she referred to as the "perfect man." She was madly in love with him.

When she went out with him, he opened the car door. When they went to a restaurant, he pulled the chair out. He told her to order whatever she wanted to eat, and not to order something she did not like. He told her that he would order the wine and if she did not like it, she could always change it. He always took her to the most expensive restaurants in town.

He used to call her twice a day and he used to see her three times a week. He told her that he had gone out with a few girls before he met her and that she was different. He told her that she was the best girl he had met. He complimented her on her beauty and told her how attracted he was to her. He told her he wanted her to meet his family, his children and his closest friends.

Three or four months passed, but she never met them.

During the week, he continued to call her and would tell her that that night they were going to go to dinner and afterward to a movie. One weekend he told her he would make a reservation and take her someplace she had never been before.

She still thought he was the most perfect man she had met in her entire life. She had fallen in love with him.

She was happy when she was with him, but when she talked with him about the future, he always changed the subject.

He was very smart, very successful, very handsome, very polite, and he had lots of money. He made her feel like she was a queen.

She threw him a surprise party for his birthday. She bought him a lot of presents and spent a lot of money.

He knew she was getting too serious. This was scary for him. After the party, he called her only once or twice a week. He did not come around much to take her out. Everything slowed way down.

Then her girlfriend called. She said to her friend that she saw her boyfriend the night before. She told her that her boyfriend and another woman were laughing and having a good time.

She was in a state of shock. She told her that it must not have been her boyfriend. It must have been someone else. She was jealous. She had even kissed him on the lips at his birthday party. She started crying like a baby. She almost went to the emergency room.

She felt that she could never trust any man again. She became down on all men. She wasn't right for a long time.

Finally she called this man. "We haven't seen each other for a long time," she told him. "I really miss you and I want to see you."

She was still so burned and so hurt that she could barely talk. She had thrown all of her heart into the relationship.

This man was still married with two children. His wife wanted to divorce him because he was now living with someone else.

A man with a lot of money can think he is entitled to do this. When a woman today makes a proposition to a man, he does not want to refuse her.

The only reason this man had this girl was to occupy his mind. She was only a convenience. He was using her.

Anytime he dated a woman, he knew how to make a woman fall in love with him. He treated her wonderfully. He knew how to manipulate a woman. Every time he took a woman out, he knew how to play that game.

The underlying reason for this was because he was broken hearted, too.

If he had been a nice man, he would have dated this woman and told her he did not want to get serious. His feelings were not there for her. He did not want anything steady. Not only that, he was married. The minute she got serious, he decided to take off.

He thought he could get away with having an affair. Then when his wife woke up and smelled the coffee, he could not believe it. He did not want a divorce.

There are men walking around like this today. They think differently than we women do. The girl had felt like she won the jackpot, but later on, he dropped a bomb on her.

Sometimes women can trust a man too much. A woman should hide her heart. Women need to learn to take things slowly. Women are sensitive and when a woman gets intimate with a man, she can get hurt easily.

We are too soft. We can't help falling in love with a man, especially when he treats us like a queen. When we get attached to a man, we can't control our feelings, and our feelings stay for a long time.

But, remember, if this happened to you, it becomes an experience. Learn from the experience. Be more careful the next time. A woman shouldn't take a man so seriously. She should only take herself seriously.

It is difficult when a woman throws all of her heart to a man who is separated. She thinks that they will be together forever. However, there will be nothing but heartbreak.

The only time a woman should get serious with a man is when he puts a ring on her finger. Or when he buys her an expensive piece of jewelry. Other than that, talk is cheap.

When a woman meets a man she thinks she might like to be with, she has to protect herself by not getting too serious and by continuing to date other men. She shouldn't give away her heart too soon. Otherwise, she makes it too easy for a man.

Men don't actually like things too easy. Men prefer a challenge. If you are looking for a long term relationship, you are defeating your purpose by getting serious too soon.

Dating Married Men with No Children

Sometimes it is okay to date a married man. He is not happy with his wife. He is bored, and it takes time for a man to get divorced.

Some men are like children. Some are like babies. They get distracted. They want you to treat them like you treat your children. The minute you don't pay attention, they're gone. These men are apt to come over a lot because they have nowhere to go.

Sometimes a man never leaves his wife because he is too comfortable. He is all set. If the wife has everything and if he has a certain lifestyle, he is not apt to leave. You can spoil him and he can spoil you. However, make sure this man pays attention to you and helps you do the things you need to do.

You cannot date one man unless he gives you a rock. You need insurance.

Get that, before you get too old.

Dating Conversation

You might be with one man and still be thinking about another man you broke up with. If you meet someone else, they will not want to hear about the other person. So avoid talking to someone in a new relationship about the other person you broke up with.

If you are on a date, it is considered bad etiquette to talk about another man. Even if the man wants to seek out information about the previous man, do not talk about him. It will cast a shadow on your relationship, even if you don't realize it. It can ruin your evening or the time you spend together.

You need to have positive conversation. You need to relate to and with each other in order to form building blocks upon which your new relationship can grow.

You can talk about your former lover with a close friend or with your psychiatrist, but avoid this topic on dates. Some men want to know all about your former relationships, marriages, and engagements. It's not necessary to tell them your dating or marital history. It is best to tell them that you would like to enjoy the time talking about your mutual interests and that those other things are in the past.

However, this could work against you in the future, even though you did not do anything wrong. It could create a stigma for you and give a man a psychological excuse not to commit to you and to remain flaky with you. It could give a man too much ammunition that can be used against you later if you have a serious discussion or an argument. Then the man's attitude can really change toward you.

Looking for a Man

If you look for a guy, you may never find him.

You could be very disappointed because you are searching too hard for love.

A woman wants to have fun, but she does not want an overnight attachment.

A woman does not need a man to take her places because she can do that herself. A woman can take herself to dinner and a movie.

It's good to go out to the movies, especially funny ones, with a man and to go to dinner with him and with friends. When you have stress, you have a lot on your mind.

When you date a new man, talk about the present and where you are going, not about the past. Talk about him.

Don't drink more than one drink because he might think you are an alcoholic. Besides, you need to stay alert. He might want to get you into bed.

After four dates with a man, if you don't like what he says, I don't think you want to see him again. If you have a lot of time, you can go on another date, but do the same as before: focus on what is important. Don't let your mind start wandering with all kinds of worries.

Don't bring a man home. Never. Go to his house. If a man doesn't bring you home after the fourth or fifth date, something is wrong. Either he has a girlfriend or he is married. Some men just can't finish what they start.

If you find a man you like, you have to know what you are doing because there's a real shortage of nice men.

Once you find him, how do you keep him around? If he takes you out more than three times, you have to cook for him. You've got to train him, too. He has to do more for you because he is a man.

There are very few nice men. Mostly there are men who go out to take a woman to bed.

Living with a Man

A woman dated a man for three years. One day he said he would never get married. It was a total shock to her.

At work one day she went to a deli for lunch. She did not know that her boyfriend was going to be there. She saw him staring so hard at the other girls there that he fell out of the chair.

She cooled off toward him and now she doesn't know if she wants a long term relationship with him or not.

Trust

It's difficult to fall in love with a man today because you don't know whether he is married, divorced (possibly with children at home), living with someone, or still attached to a former love. Before you go out, you ought to know him better.

We, as women, get hurt more easily than men do because we are sensitive. A man can find a woman and the next day it does not seem to phase him. He can detach himself easily. It is not the same with women.

He may even know somebody else he is interested in before he decides to leave. It's a back up system some men have.

When anybody gets hurt, they are reluctant to go out with someone again because they might get hurt again.

Men can go to many different places and meet many different women.

A man can say anything to you.

Remember: talk is cheap.

Determining if a Man is Using You

You can tell if a man is just using you.

How do you know that?

Ask yourself these questions: Does what he tells you match up with his actions? Does he help you with the basic things you need? Does he sincerely care for you and take you seriously? Does he ask you questions about yourself and is he really interested in knowing who you are?

Don't let a man just come over and eat your food and dirty your bed. Make him take you out.

Don't let him treat you like a cheap bottle of wine.

When a man talks about other women he was once with, it is very distressing. A woman does not want to know a man's history with other women. She doesn't want to that rubbed in her face. When a man talks about his past, his wife, his kids, it makes you feel like an outsider. You wonder what you are doing with him. You can only sit there and try to grin and bear it.

If you really like a man, you have to train him to be the way you want him to be. He is capable of reaching for the moon for you. Everything he owns will be yours if he really loves you. That's a real man for you. You are the center of his life. Without you, he feels he does not exist.

If a man does not like your child, you have to break up with him. If a man cares for you, he will love you even though you have four or five kids. If he is a good man, he will try hard to get to know your child and help you raise and put the child through school.

He will show you how much he loves you and that he is willing to do things for you. This kind of man has education, good values and a good background. That is a real man. If a man cannot be trained within a certain time, you have to decide what to do. You cannot spend too much time on a man who is not going to produce. But you have to do your part, too. If you don't do your part, he is going to walk away. You don't have to kill yourself, but you have to do something. You have to try to make him happy.

Men Who are Control Freaks

When you find a man like this, it will not necessarily be that obvious at first. He can learn how to blend in and act like the guy next door and still be very controlling in his behavior. You have to really give this time. It's all part of getting to know a man and finding out how he will act in given situations.

Once you get to know him, you can decide whether or not you want to deal with him and whether or not he is worth it. But you are not going to change him. I guarantee that.

If a man is a control freak, he is jealous, possessive. He might be overly clean, obsessive and compulsive.

He is not a control freak by accident. There is a reason for his behavior.

First of all, he has no patience. Second of all, he has nothing better to do. Third, his actions are based on a projection of his own behavior. If he is jealous, it is because he can't be trusted.

His behavior is learned from his mother. He is a fanatic. He is excessively nervous. He is neurotic. He is usually a lazy person.

Nothing you do is ever good enough. You know that the best you can do with this man is to let him do everything.

He is a master of deception. At the onset he tells that you he loves you and that he is willing to do anything for you. He tells you that he will pamper you.

Then the truth gradually comes out. What is revealed is a monster, a tyrant.

Dating Someone You Work With

If you choose to date someone you work with, beware!

You have to swear this person to secrecy. This should be kept strictly confidential.

Don't forget. This place of work is your livelihood. Finding another job out there is not that easy, especially if you're over thirty or forty.

The problem is, among other things, that if you stop dating, then the other people at work can start to mind your business for you. They can make your life absolutely miserable. And some will, given the opportunity.

If you choose to get serious, it might be a different story. You have to find out what the work policies are. In some places, if you date or marry someone, they terminate you. That consequence could be devastating.

So it is only with this stern caveat that you do so: Date someone you work with at your own risk.

You should try to avoid dating anyone you work with. But, if you do, be discreet. You don't want to be the main topic of conversation at the office.

Dating a Man with Children

If a man has two or three kids, it is doubtful whether he has time for you.

The problem is that he cannot bring you into the family life until he knows you. He has to be able to trust you with the kids. It's hard.

If you have problems, he is not likely to have the time for you because he has the young children to deal with. However, he might think you are sitting there waiting for him, and you could be left out in the cold waiting for him.

You can also be so jealous that you are not going to know what to do.

If you have grown kids, you do not want to start all over again.

You can't have any feelings for his kids. If you get attached to the kids and you don't see him anymore, then you are going to be very hurt.

Sometimes men don't think. If you have a date with a man, he will postpone it if his kids are sick.

If a man has children, he might not have much money. He might not be able to afford even a movie, dinner, or flowers. He might not want to buy you flowers because he feels it is a waste of money. This makes a relationship difficult.

Time is short. You have to decide if this man is for you or not.

Children

A man must be nice to your kids.

If not, then you shouldn't go out with him even though you like him very much. It isn't going to work. The relationship will fall apart.

You have to teach your kids how to behave towards a man who's not their father. The mother has to do that.

If you date a man and he has kids, but he does not introduce you to them, you should not go out with him. Eventually he will not go out with you any more. He's looking for other people. It's a waste of your time. He may even be thinking he will go back with his wife, especially if the kids are younger. It's too complicated.

If the kids are grown, it's different.

Single Mothers Living With Men

You cannot be too lenient with children, but on the same token, you cannot be too strict. If you are too lenient, then the children will think they can get away with everything. If you are too strict, they will be apt to rebel.

You need to discipline them, but you also need to explain why you feel the way you do and the reason for the discipline. Sometimes they don't get it right away, but it comes to them later on, when they get to be thirty-something.

You have to be very careful about the friends and the men you bring home and the influence that they can have on your children. Remember that they don't necessarily have your children's best interests at heart. If it's a male friend, you have to supervise them, especially your daughters, so they aren't corrupted or taken advantage of.

Living Together Unmarried and Having Children

If you meet someone, start living together, and then have a baby without getting married, the child is going to feel as if he has no father, even if the father is living there. The couple should get married before the child is aware of the situation.

When these children grow up and get to be teenagers, they are going to emulate their parents. They will be going out with someone, then living with them and having a baby without getting married. They are going to do the same things you did.

This starts problems for the parents and the child, and these will not be small problems, but big problems. It's not healthy for anyone involved.

Sometimes other children will make fun of the child and say that they don't have a father. Children should not have to listen to anything so unpleasant when they are little.

The situation is not right. If the mother is taking care of the house and the child and the father every day, she is frustrated. She is not settled. She is not happy. A wife who is a mother needs roots. She needs to be solid as a parent.

What if something happens to the father? The mother has to be protected so she does not have to worry about how she is going to feed the children. Otherwise, it is the children who suffer. The parents have to realize this. If they do otherwise, they are not thinking properly. They are not thinking about the child or about themselves because the consequences could be drastic with insurance, health benefits, money, college, and other issues.

Whatever the man has—the house, bank accounts, stocks, and so forth—should be in both the mother's and the father's names. The mother should know everything that is going on with these accounts, and there should be two different lawyers—one for the mother and one for the father—to draw up papers that protect the mother and the children.

If a mother is not going to get married, then in no time she'll open her eyes and she'll be over forty. Then who is going to marry her? It's difficult to answer this. After fifty, it is even harder to get married.

A woman has to find a career. Otherwise she has no goals. All she has is a kid. When you have children, you can't just live for the moment. You have to think of the long term.

One Relationship

Some women are in one relationship in which they get burned and then they have trouble re-connecting with a man again. They can become so hurt and wounded that it is very difficult for them to trust a man again. Women get hurt much more easily than men do.

A woman needs to hide her emotions to a certain degree until she really gets to know a man. If a woman lets a man get away with too much, then he will take her for granted.

Vested Interest

A man you have seen for a while needs to have vested his interest in you if he is expected to stay. This is a woman's insurance policy. He needs to buy you a piece of jewelry or a ring and not expect you to give it back. If you break up after the two of you have spent time together, a woman should not have to give it back. She invested her time in him, and if they were engaged and the engagement is over, she may have been humiliated. The ring becomes a small consolation at that point.

You have to buy a man presents sometimes, too.

When You Fall in Love

You have been going out with a man for a long time. Neither one of you says, "I love you" to the other. But you are in love with each other.

This man talks about his mother. His mother may have said to her son, "Hide your heart because a woman could hurt you." Some men really listen to their mother. This man is set in his ways and you won't be able to change him. He will find a wife that resembles his mother and that his mother approves of.

Sometimes a mother is never happy with her son's friends or girlfriends. Meantime she is ruining her son. He is going to live with his mother forever. He does not have to spend a lot of money because his mother does it all. He is never going to leave his nest.

This kind of relationship is very difficult for the girl. No matter what, she really wants to spend her time with this person, but she can't change him. She is better off moving on.

Are You Alone on the Weekends?

If a man does not go out with you on a Saturday or if he does not call you on a weekend, something is wrong. Do not delude yourself.

If he sees you only once a week, that's no good either.

Meanwhile he is out there doing monkey business.

Soul Mate

Soul mates come together when they have similar interests and a mutual need to be together. It is as if they were designed to be with each other. The relationship is more than just an arrangement to handle loneliness.

You can finish each other's sentences without even trying. You know what the other one is thinking. You let each other have the space and privacy necessary after a long day. You don't need to have raging arguments to communicate. You have a peaceful stream of communication and are supportive of each other.

Finding your soul mate is not impossible. Don't get discouraged. However, it is not that common that couples are soul mates.

If you find your soul mate, it is truly wonderful. But if not, you will not be doomed to being alone for the rest of your life. You can still manage to find a person to be involved with in a meaningful relationship even if they are not your soul mate. It will just be different—not necessarily less happy, just different.

The main thing we are looking for in a relationship is happiness.

We are trying to find someone who knows how to respond to our needs, either naturally or with some coaching or "training," if you will. If a man needs a little training to satisfy your needs, don't necessarily think you have to reject him right off the bat. If you are patient enough and he is willing and has a good attitude, then it might be worth the attempt. However, if he needs a lot of training or doesn't seem to listen, it might be so frustrating that it becomes too much of a chore to make it work successfully.

Don't try to force a relationship. It will never work. Don't go overboard in the relationship. But it depends on what he does for you, too, and sometimes it depends on what the man is looking for. You should not be a slave yourself, though.

You don't want to get hurt. Don't get your hopes up too high. Just be ready to go on. Don't feel sorry for yourself. That's the worst thing you can do.

Don't take a man who has to be with you all the time. If you let this happen and then you break up, where does that leave you when all of your time has been for him? You will be left hanging. When they are gone, where are you? They find someone right away. You are the one that may be left hurting and alone.

If a relationship does not work out, don't think you are failing because in the future, if it kept going, it would be unpleasant. Don't hang onto a man too long if you are not happy because time goes on quickly. You may have to move on, but don't be angry with yourself. You are doing yourself a favor.

The main thing you have to remember is to separate the wheat from the chaff. Remember to get rid of the pretenders.

If someone does not enhance your life, they detract from it. You want someone who can be your life partner, who will work with you to help you get what you want, not just someone who emotionally bleeds you dry to the point that you have nothing left to give to anyone else.

Implement caution, time and courage and be patient enough to wait for someone to support and help you grow as the unique person you are

If a man is not invested in you, then he is apt to walk away at any time. Nothing is holding him there. The reason why he has not invested in you is because he wants to keep his options open. He can walk away with anyone else he happens to find. This is not uncommon. Don't take it personally. This is just the way it is.

If you want to, you can hint to him about buying you a nice piece of jewelry. See what he says. Listen carefully because it will tell you everything.

If a man really cares for you, he won't take a long time to know it and he'll ask you to marry him within three months. Otherwise, he'll get spoiled.

Love and Sex

Some men can easily profess their love for you when they want to go to bed with you. Then they get amnesia after the fact.

These men will be affectionate up to that point, and after, when they want sex, they will be so sweet with you again. After sex, they get cold and become different people. They act like they don't know you.

Some men do not know what love is all about. They're confused between love and sex. They take ten minutes to think about it. That kind of relationship is not going to last. Sooner or later they will find someone other than you.

These men are going to take all your energy and drain you. They are going to confuse you. These men are not reliable. They do not consider your feelings.

Don't let this relationship last too long because they can hurt you terribly. Watch out because you must save yourself. Don't let yourself get hurt.

You must know what you want from a man. You probably want a man because you want a serious and intimate relationship. When you're young and you meet a guy and get to know him, you have to be careful not to go out with him for a long time or you'll forget yourself and your goals. One day, you'll wake up and suddenly smell the coffee.

Americans talk a lot with sexual innuendo. When you first meet someone, he'll sometimes talk about sex. Only once you've known each other for a while should you talk about sex and then it should come about naturally.

In America, men start to have sexual relations in their early teens. Parents often start to give birth control to their children out of fear that they will get pregnant or impregnate someone else. Then, from age twenty on, their children begin to think more seriously about their life. They calm down and start to get interested in getting married. They begin to mature into relationships with one another.

No one can expect a man to remain exactly the same as when you first met him. You might feel neglected by your husband because he watches football on the weekends, he plays golf, and he hangs around with his buddies and leaves you at home by yourself. Sometimes he might forget your birthday or wedding anniversary and you take that as a sign that he no longer cares about you.

But this is life.

Dating a Married Man with Children

She knows that he is married, and so they always have arguments. She wants him to leave his wife, but he knows that if he keeps the girlfriend around, he is going to ruin his children's life.

Italian men especially are loyal to their wives. Some of them like to have mistresses, but they are also loyal to their kids. They like to raise their kids and put them through college. Their girlfriends eventually fly the coop even though these men can be very sweet to their girlfriends and the girlfriends have thought that they would do anything for them. But they don't.

Sometimes if a man can't get something from his wife, he will seek out someone else. A wife's job lasts twenty-four hours a day. His does not. His job is only eight hours long. Husbands don't realize that when their wives go out to work and come home, they are really just switching gears to the second shift. They are really still at work, but at a different job. It is non-stop. It's not easy to work to take care of a husband, kids, and a house. It's a continuous juggling act.

Mother Obsession

Some men simply worship their mothers. They may not be happy unless they find someone like their mother or someone who reminds them of their mother.

"Male Chauvinist Pigs"

Are there "male chauvinist pigs"? Probably a couple.

These men take women to expensive dinners to get sex. They're looking not for a relationship, but for a conquest. This is especially true of older men who were raised to think of women as property. They think they should keep you at home as a convenience to clean their house and to have sex with. They don't treat you like a woman. They think they are smart, but they are not, because in the end they are the ones who lose.

Communication

You both need to communicate when you have a problem. You both have to talk about it. When you have a problem, it's not a good idea to hold back.

You could even try to set an appointment with your spouse so you are not too busy with everything else going on around you. Don't do anything when you cannot concentrate. Otherwise, you could make a mistake or you could hurt each other's feelings.

You want your marriage to be successful so it's important to do things together. Try to do projects in which you have equal participation. If you are both working outside of the home, you have to help each other when you get home. If you work together, you can work faster than if you work separately. That way you can both feel good doing things together as a team, and you are more productive and faster.

This kind of relationship can actually start from the moment two people first become attracted to each other. It manifests itself in a body language signifying a desire to become more intimate with each other. It includes holding hands and an exchange of sweet words. Special relationships consist of both sexual and emotional levels that you share together.

Too often a sexual relationship can settle down to the "basics," where sexual arousal techniques are focused purely toward intercourse and orgasm while the subtle expressions of love and tenderness, such as kissing, are regularly overlooked. Let kissing remain an important part of your physical interaction outside the bedroom as well as an integral part of your foreplay and lovemaking.

The moments immediately after making love can create problems in a relationship. Quite clearly, both have needs which must be met, but if a man consistently "turns off" after orgasm, his partner is likely to construe his actions as a sign that he does not care about her. His behavior may render the whole sexual experience null and void for her, and she may feel bitterly rejected.

Holding on to a Man

When things are too good, some men become too comfortable. When tough times come along, they could split off.

Other men will be grateful when things are comfortable.

It is difficult to know how to be with a man when his behavior is unpredictable, but you do have to present a challenge to a man.

Men need excitement.

Men as Friends

It's nice to have men as friends.

It depends on what you are looking for, soul mate, companion or husband.

Men can be very good friends. If you are looking for a friend, find the kind of man who does not go out with too many girlfriends. He's loyal.

Sometimes you can act like boyfriend and girlfriend. Mentally, he can think you are his girlfriend, but you are not. He will never ask you to go to bed, though, unless you want to.

You are comfortable with this person. You can talk about your past if you want to. Some men are sensitive, and they will forever be your friends. If you want to go out with someone just for sex, you could do that if you and he like. It's healthy and no questions are asked. It can be a flexible relationship, no strings attached, or it can also be platonic, just friends.

Dating a Man over 50 Who Has Never Been Married

You must realize that a man like this is very comfortable with himself and set in his ways. If you see him too much, he'll get frustrated. He is only used to dealing with himself.

If he likes you, however, he can be trained, but it takes a long time. He is not apt to change very much at first because he is scared. He is afraid of you and doesn't know what to do with you, but he will have a very sensitive side.

Sometimes he is very neat. Everything has to be in order. You have to work around him in that respect.

This man will not be pushy to get physical. He won't try to get you to do anything that you don't want to do.

He might get you frustrated actually because he doesn't seem to know how to treat a woman. It might be too taxing for you if you have to tell him what to do every step of the way.

On the other hand, a man like this can also learn how to cook. Try to save money with him. Shop wisely. Eat home sometimes. Save money for a rainy day.

This kind of relationship is such that he can be a reliable man for a woman. It depends on what kind of man you are looking for. He could be a nice person to be with, but this relationship might take a little while to work out.

Once there was a woman who dated a man for a while. She was a daddy's princess and she was looking for a man who treated her just like her father did.

The man she was dating told her from the beginning that he was too old to get married and too old to have children. He kept warning her, but he liked to go out with her. He did everything for her until she was not capable of doing anything for herself.

One day she got pregnant anyway, in spite of what he told her. When she told him that she was pregnant, he told her to get an abortion. She did.

She was forty years old and she never had had a child before, but she wanted one. She felt terrible afterward. They broke up.

As long as she lived, she never forgave herself. She cried for years. Her eyes were always red. She was on anti-depressants. She could not cope with it.

Sometimes, when a woman has an abortion, she can never get pregnant again.

Male Insecurities

There was a man who thought that all that was important was sex. Without sex, he did not know what to do. He thought that sex was everything.

He was empty inside and outside, and he had made it this way for himself. He was a very lonely man. He would never have anybody.

At a certain age, a man should no longer do this. Everybody will run away from him. A man like this has no clue what life is all about.

Sex is beautiful, if the two of you love each other. If you have no feelings for one another, sex is dirty.

Look at the Man Inside

Some women insist that there are no men out there.

While this is partially true, you must be willing to overlook superficial things when looking for a man. When you are dating a man, you must remember that some men don't care how they look. They don't present themselves well. Don't just look at their appearance.

Look to the inner spirit of the man.

For example, a man could be wealthy and not know how to dress. Sometimes a man dresses wonderfully and doesn't have any money, or at least refuses to spend it on you.

You have to give yourself time to get to know a man to find out how he really is inside. You each need time to get to know each other. A lot of people judge a book by the cover, but with men you should not do that.

You can always help him with his clothes later on if you really like him. Some men don't like to dress up. They insist that you take them exactly the way they are. They resist change, but do not fear. If they really like you, in time, they will change the way they dress.

When a woman meets a man, she must let him like her first. After that she should still respond, however, with caution. If he looks too perfect, other women will likely be after him. If he is too neat or too clean, he can drive you crazy because he is so compulsive. You will have to work very hard to constantly please this man.

You must get to know a man to see if you can tolerate living with his behavior.

Just Living with a Man

Before you live together, everything looks good.

Afterward, a man can't hide anymore.

Couples start all over when they live together. A woman must know a man well in order to live together.

There was a woman who met a man who said he wanted to get married. As soon as they started living together, he started drinking and acting up. He was a totally different person than he had been before.

She walked out on him.

When a couple decides to live together without the benefit of marriage, it is a good idea for them to have a cohabitation agreement with respect to financial responsibilities, duties regarding the arrangement and division of possessions if they split up, and anything else which is pertinent. To protect themselves they should make sure any titles or leases they have are in both names. This holds true if they have a Cohabitation Agreement as well. They should each use a different attorney for their part of the agreement, too.

Dating a Man for 8-10 Years

If you have been dating a man for eight to ten years, you might start to think you are wasting your time. You might start to realize that, if he wanted, he could drop you like a hot potato. Then where would you be?

You are getting old. Why would you be living together so long without getting married? You have nothing to look forward to.

I knew a woman who had plastic surgery so she could make herself look young. Don't you think she felt bad trying so hard to look young? A man doesn't need to look young, if he has money. This woman let a man take advantage of her, but she did let him do it. If you have a man who's a smooth talker, you have to watch it.

If you have lived with a man for a long time, give him a deadline for marriage. You have worked hard to please him for all of these years. Otherwise you could see your life evaporate right before your eyes.

Men You Don't Know

Sometimes when you start to date a man, you need to do a background check on him. You have to know where he works, how long he has worked there, and where he lives. Call up his employer. Find out something about him.

There was a woman whose husband had died. She lived in an extremely nice home. One evening she met a man in a nightclub. She had seen him there regularly, but she had never been introduced to him before.

The man started seeing her. They were always going dancing and going out to dinner.

He told her that he had sold his house and that he made a lot of money from the sale. He had cash, he said, and he wanted to put the money in her deposit box.

He put his cash in her safe deposit box, and told her that he wanted the code to the box in the event that she were to go away.

When she came home from work one day, she found everything in her deposit box gone.

Younger Men with Older Women

This type of woman may mix younger men and older men. She likes to go out with younger men because she likes to play and be very active. And she wants her freedom. She does not want to be cooped up with anyone. She does not want to live with anyone.

She feels that gay guys are very nice to be with. It's like having a son or a girlfriend.

This woman is very attractive. She keeps herself looking well. She eats well and exercises regularly. She doesn't eat any junk food. Doesn't smoke. Doesn't drink. Her goal is to enjoy life.

There was a woman named Jennifer who met a man who had been married three times. His first wife had three kids with him as the father. He was married to his second wife, but had no children from that marriage. He married his third wife for love. She already had four kids and he wanted to take care of her and the kids. He left because she was older than he was and because she was not affectionate with him.

Jennifer wanted to meet an older man and she did.

He thought she was beautiful. He told her that he was in the process of getting a divorce. He wanted to be with Jennifer and the feelings were mutual.

She went one day to his hotel room to talk to him and to get to know him better. He wanted her to jump into bed with him immediately.

He was too anxious to recapture what he had in his marriages. He was too quick. He wanted instant gratification.

If you keep dating this kind of man, they will suck out all of your energy. There will be nothing left to you.

Jennifer left him there in the motel. The next morning they got together to have breakfast. She had lost interest. He told that he would like to see her again, but she said "Good-bye."

All she wanted was to meet a nice guy who didn't push the issue of a sexual encounter, which is what was on the foremost part of this other man's mind. It was a big turn off.

When this man gave her his phone numbers, he only gave her the office numbers. When a man only gives you his work number, you should be suspicious. Use your common sense.

Men over 50 Who Have Never Been Married

This man is not easy to be around. He thinks he is too old to start something new.

You would like to be around him because you think he can make your life easy, but it would be difficult to be in a relationship with this man. He enjoys having the companionship, but he is not looking for a committed relationship.

Sometimes his parents left this kind of man a lot of money. He's afraid of getting married because he does not want to part with the money he has. He would rather be alone. He dates, but he does not want to get married.

People do strange things when they have money. They feel more comfortable finding someone who has as much money as they do. They are always busy with themselves because they have houses in different places. They don't go in with just everyone. They always hang around their own kind.

They might not always show that they have money, especially when you look at them. They may wear plain clothing, but they'll drive an expensive car.

Men who Never Complain

This man is polite and he could be well educated. He may come from a comfortable background. He could be sensitive.

When he has a problem, he will never discuss it with anyone except his mother. Sometimes this man likes to talk to his mother because she will give him the right advice and she has been around more than he has. This man could be a good husband, but he will find a wife as a mother figure.

He likes to go expensive places and he will likely do the same thing his parents did. If you become a friend of this person, he will not jump to any conclusions as to what he wants you to do. If you do a little thing, he will appreciate it very much. He's kind of a quiet person with sincere affections.

This man does not like anything to be too complicated.

This man needs a lot of love.

A woman has to be educated to be with this man. He has high standards for the woman he wants to share his life with. You have to think before you open your mouth because he is so sensitive. Be careful.

Some men don't know how to handle their anger. Some men are apt to complain a lot. Some men are stressed. They are doing too many different things at one time, and they never finish what they start. Some men are too wound up at the office. They should start one thing and finish it completely before they go on to the next. There is stress coming in because they are doing too many things at once. They come home and they are still are stressed because they did not finish what they were doing at work.

A man should not complain and take his anger out on his wife. If he can't control his anger, he should work quietly until he is finished what he is doing. He should never show his anger and he should control his temper. He should be pleasant, even if it is hard or even if he is sad. A man should be able to take anything, whether he is down or up or sad.

When a little thing goes wrong, a man should never lose his temper. A woman will not want to go to bed with him that night. She will lose her affection and emotion for him.

A woman can work hard and cook dinner. The man might come home and not like his wife's cooking. A wife's job is hard, but a wife is not her husband's keeper. He should remember that.

A husband must be patient. He should think about what he says before he says it. If a man opens his mouth too fast, he could hurt his wife.

Dating a Man of a Different Race

There was a mixed race couple who went out for several years. He gave her an engagement ring, but he did not tell his parents he was giving her a ring. He just went and did it. His parents started interfering then because they got nervous that the woman was actually going to marry him. On special occasions, such as his birthday and on holidays, she would not go with the man to celebrate at his parents' house.

Parents are sometimes unhappy with the partner their child selects.

These parents made it very unpleasant for this woman. They weakened the relationship. His parents told him that if he married this woman, they would disinherit him. The parents broke them up even though he had been dating this woman for a few years.

He became so lonely that he finally married someone else of his same ethnic background.

Then he became terribly unhappy and terribly sorry that he did not marry his true love. She had by that time met someone else and fallen in love, but he wanted her back badly. He was remorseful, but she did not want him anymore because he had hurt her so.

Parents, as well as children, can be mean when they try to dictate who a person is supposed to be with. The person then can wind up making a wrong decision because of the strong influence that the relatives have. A life can be forever ruined.

Single Woman who is Divorced with Children

When I started dating men, my daughter was probably three or four and was very active. I couldn't relax. Some men thought my child was in the way. They were not too happy.

If a man didn't like my daughter, I would not keep him because he would not be able to enjoy being with us. He wouldn't be happy.

If the man really cares for you and he loves you, he's going to treat the kids just like his kids. He will act like a real man and will treat your kids nicely.

When he is first dating, the man will feel funny. The children might be jealous of him. Likewise, the man might be jealous of the children. The children could deliberately ruin the relationship. Sometimes, they might come right out and say, "You can't marry that man."

You have to explain to children that it is important to try to accept this man and integrate him into their lives. If a man really loves a woman, he will just jump in there and help take care of your children. Children like to have a man around the house because it gives them security.

Some men love to have children around the house. This can work well, provided you train the children and the man to be cooperative together. Communication is key for true caring for one another.

Falling in Love with Two Men at One Time

There was a woman who met a man on a train. She was commuting to work in Manhattan. They saw each other every morning, but they did not talk for a long time. Sometimes they would sit next to each other. She was a little older than he was.

Eventually, they spoke to each other. He asked her to go have a drink, and she went with him. They didn't exchange phone numbers. They saw each other again, but always on the train. They talked about themselves and what they did for a living.

One day he did ask her for her phone number. He was quite a bit younger than she was, so she didn't think anything about it. She had a fleeting thought in a romantic direction, but she didn't think there would be any future for them as a couple so she dismissed any idea of having a romance with him.

Then he called her and asked her to go to dinner. She would not go. She didn't want to get confused, mainly because of the age difference. She did find him attractive because he was tall and handsome and she did enjoy his company when she saw him on the train; but she did not think she would fit into his life

Two years went by and he still was asking her to go out with him. She finally agreed to go out to dinner with him. She wanted to be with him and to spend more time with him, but after their dinner, she backed off.

Meanwhile she had another male friend whom she dated platonically. He too was younger. She saw this man two or three times a week. They would go to dinner and sometimes they would go away together. They just enjoyed each other's company. They were very good friends.

Five more years went by and the man on the train was still interested in this woman. They saw each other on the way to work during the week, but everything else remained the same.

He still called her to ask her out. She would go out to dinner and to the movies with him. She kept the relationship very light and at arm's length because she had been seeing the other man from the start and more often.

The man on the train stopped calling her for a while. For about two years they did not even see each other on the train. She was happy not to hear from him because she did not want him to interrupt her relationship with her other male friend.

After the two years went by she saw him again, and he told her that he had gotten married and that he now had children.

This confused her. At first she felt relieved because she knew that he wouldn't be calling her anymore. On the other hand, she felt a loss from the finality of the situation and from knowing that she would miss him. She felt lonely inside. She had never been aware of how lonely she was before this happened.

Even though he had married, he would still call her to say hello. But they did not see each other. They felt very comfortable with each other just having conversations together on the phone. They could say anything to one another.

Three more years went by and one day he called her and told her he had gotten a divorce. He seemed lonely to her. He kept calling her. They started seeing each other again on the train, just as before. They saw each other for dinner or drinks from time to time too.

One day they each felt lonely. They went to have dinner and they gave each other a romantic kiss goodnight. They started to get warmer feelings toward one another. She felt she had to resist, but she had strong feelings to be with him.

He finally asked her, "Will you go away with me on a vacation for two weeks?"

She told him no, because she had to work. While he was on vacation, he called her almost every day to join him there. He was within driving distance and he gave her directions how to get there.

A week after he had left, she went by herself to join him at a resort in Martha's Vineyard. When she arrived there it was late, but he was glad to see her and they went to dinner together. He was so warm toward her. She felt attracted to him because he was an unusual person and excellent company.

They slept together that night.

She did not tell him, but she was not satisfied. She was in tears because she had been waiting all these years to be with him.

She tried again the next morning, but there was the same result. She was very upset. This situation repeated itself several times during the week that they were away together. It became worse for her because she was so disappointed and let down. It ruined her vacation, but he was not aware of how badly she felt. She was crying, but she didn't really let him see.

They came home together and he went his way and she went hers. They still talked with each other, but they did not see each other for a month after that.

Then he called her to get together, and she decided to see him again. She had talked with her girlfriend and told her what happened. Her girlfriend suggested seeing him again to see how things would go. So she got together with him again for dinner, and they spent the night together.

Unfortunately, nothing had changed.

He knew at this point that she was unhappy, and they did not see each other after that.

Sometimes when a man wants to be intimate with you, he is so nervous, it only takes him four minutes and he's satisfied.

Sometimes his mind is someplace else. Men don't necessarily know how a woman feels. They might not even ask a woman if she had an orgasm. Some men are either inconsiderate or they don't have a clue.

It is important that a woman have an orgasm. You have to find someone you can match. If you go buy a pair of gloves, for example, in order for you to feel comfortable in them, they have to fit you. Otherwise, they are no good to you.

It is sometimes hard for a woman to find a man she is attracted to and who fits.

If you really want a man around, and if you have the time and patience, you might be able to teach him what to do. Sometimes, though, men are too mechanical and are unemotional. If you have known a man for a long time, you hope that when you are intimate with him it will work out, but you really don't know whether it will work out until you actually are intimate him. That is the only way to know what kind of chemistry the two of you are going to have together.

The woman finally stopped seeing the man from the train after their intimate relationship didn't work out. She had still been dating her other male friend. They would go to dinner and movies together, but there was no romance with him. They remained friends for a long time.

Sometimes he would joke and say he was going to buy her an engagement ring. Other times he would joke and say he would not have sex until he got married. They continued to go out, but still only as friends. This was peculiar.

He was very religious. His parents were rich and had a different background than other people. He did not have much of a social life, and he had not had many girlfriends. He lived a quiet life and worked long hours.

These two helped each other financially, too. They talked about living together, but nothing happened. They still live separately, even though they talk about marriage.

They have known each other for about eight years now. She doesn't think marriage is a good idea for her because she is older than he is. Sometimes she wants to quit the relationship because she feels there is no future together. Yet she feels sorry for him because he has difficulty making new friends, and she knows that he has feelings for her. She knows, too, that he thinks their relationship is going to be long term, if not forever. They still live in their own apartments, and they are not really close together yet

Only sometimes if you have a male friend can you stay close, perhaps forever, and keep it platonic and still love him.

This woman was confused, too, because the age difference was significant and because their backgrounds were dramatically different. Sometimes their age difference bothered her a lot.

They call each other twice a day. They see each other in the evening and on the weekends. But they each have their freedom and maybe this does add to the success of the relationship. They care for each other, but they are not sure if they are going to be intimate with each other.

When they go out, most of the time he pays the check. Sometimes he buys her presents, and sometimes he sends flowers to her office.

She doesn't try to force him to do things she wants him to do, but sometimes she teases him and says, "Why don't you watch a pornographic movie?"

But he's not interested. He is too wound up with his different jobs.

CHAPTER IV
LOVE AND MARRIAGE

Marriage

In order to have a successful marriage, you need to be able to interact with each other in a way that is mutually satisfying, yet which respects the needs and desires of each partner.

A husband may bring the needed judgment and the decision making power to the marriage. His wife may, in turn, bring kindness, softness, gentleness, and socialization into his life.

Individual privacy is an important aspect of a marriage, and the two partners may wish to retain it. While the plight of human existence is loneliness, this together-yet-separate aspect of a marriage may ensure the viability of the marriage.

The happiest marriages are those where both parties marry because they are best of friends. Many people wait to get married so that they can find a partner they trust and they truly want to be with, as a lover and as a friend.

One factor that sometimes leads to divorce is when middle aged men have perceived their wives as their mothers. This is known as the Oedipus Complex. However, no woman can ever be as good as a man's mother.

These men then turn to younger women. It's also known as macho ego because they think they are going to miss out on something. They see a younger woman with no wrinkles and they want to fulfill their mental fantasies by feeling as if that smooth skin is going to rub off on them.

A couple has to live together for at least seven years for a common law marriage to take legal effect. Only then is a woman likely to get half the man's money. If he hides his money, she has to find out where in the house he keeps it and whether he gives it to his children or not. A woman has to keep her eyes wide open. She has to do her homework.

Some states do not recognize common law marriage, but there may be other ways to get around the law by attempting to get the marriage validated by challenging it in the court system on a case-by-case basis. Be certain not to sign any documents that a man might give you unless you have a trusted, competent lawyer who has been informed of your situation. Be certain also never to use the same attorney as the man. That could damage you in many ways, but especially financially. To find a good lawyer either go to the Martindale and Hubbel's reference manual or get referrals from friends for well respected and competent lawyers.

After you get a divorce, it is almost impossible to re-open the judgment to get more money. Once you get your alimony or your lump sum payment, that's it. Do not expect one penny more.

Try to think things through carefully beforehand even though you are bound to be upset at that time. Remember he might not care if you are thrown into the street with nothing.

Don't do crazy things. Don't go taking drugs and don't go drinking. Do everything in moderation. Don't fall prey, either, to another man's advances because he senses your vulnerability. That kind of man will take advantage of you, if allowed. You can become an easy target.

Remember, it is not woman's society. It's man's society. Most of the courts favor the man, unless you have a good tough lawyer.

The above things are important for any woman getting a divorce, but if you and your spouse are in an upper income bracket, there can be even more extreme financial consequences for each of you. If you have a joint checking or savings accounts, be certain to have your lawyer freeze the accounts. Attach any property by filing a lis pendens in the town hall where the property is located. Try to get your name on everything jointly. You have to know about all the property he has solely in his name and where it is located. Some money could be hidden in a Swiss bank.

It is important not to date any other men prior to the filing of the divorce papers. After that, it is not relevant. However, you should still be careful what you do. Be discreet. You need to have a lot of energy and to be alert. Your husband could have someone following you. Be on guard. Be squeaky clean in everything you do.

It's important not to take a vacation. Your husband could go clean the house out and put everything in storage. I've seen this happen to a woman. Also, it makes you look too financially independent.

Be low-keyed in everything you do, including shopping. Keep it to the bare minimum. Pay cash for everything you buy so that it cannot be easily traced. Be certain the house is in your name, too, or he could evict you in housing court. If he makes more money than you do, you ought to consider if it is to your benefit financially to continue working. Consult your lawyer or your financial advisor.

Unfortunately, in a divorce the person who can hurt you the most is the one who loves you.

Keeping Romance Alive

Just because you have gotten to know each other, don't take the relationship for granted. Don't let the romance of those early days begin to slide.

Continue to look for ways to show your feelings. Get a present when you next meet, for example. This could be a simple token of affection and not an expensive gift laden with expectations, as though you expected something in return.

A few manners go a long way in life. They are like nurturing a plant with water. Showing thoughtfulness is important.

Give red flowers to show love and yellow to show friendship or parental care. Flowers symbolizing friendship should be mixed colors. In the Orient, we never send white flowers unless we want to say good-bye. You don't have to wait in a relationship to send flowers, either. If a woman gets even a single flower, it can be very romantic. It does not have to be a special occasion. Flowers are symbolic, and the color that signifies love more than any other is red.

A woman should play her part, too, in the art of wooing by presenting the man with little gifts such as a bottle of his favorite fragrance or of his favorite wine. This will show him her interest in learning about him and his tastes.

Showing your consideration and awareness of the other person's moods and feelings is very important. For example, when a man helps a woman with her coat or compliments her on her hair or dress, this makes a woman feel good. It shows he cares. If you notice that your friend is sick or tired after a busy day at the office, you might have an early dinner for her or gracefully let her out of the plans for the evening. That person will appreciate your consideration and your being so finely attuned to her wavelength.

It is important for a couple to do different things together and not always do the same things. You don't want your partner to get bored.

Be happy to show your partner off in public so he knows that you are proud to be with him. You should walk around together, holding hands in public and kissing. Keep the romance alive.

For a man it is important that after a nice evening together, you call her and tell her it was a nice evening. This alleviates any nagging doubts she may have developed overnight about the success of your first date. Call her at other, unexpected times to show her that you have been thinking of her and that you're still impressed with her.

Recognizing Your Need for Privacy

At different times people need privacy. Privacy is a fundamental need, and although it's the opposite of the other fundamental need, social contact, it is equally important. Everyone needs downtime to relax and to meditate, especially people who have excessively busy lives.

Everyone's needs are different and their needs may vary at different times, too, during their lives. Structure your time and your activities according to your needs. You need to keep your energies balanced within your being.

You should schedule the time you spend together in a qualitative way. Sometimes a couple will be out of synch with one another. Their energy will not feel right. They will be at odds with one another.

It is important to recognize at these times what is happening between the two of you. You need time to unwind from work and from the daily vicissitudes of life. It is all part of being able to compromise, being happy about what you are doing, and being fulfilled.

Married to a Younger Man

A woman feels good when she dates a younger man. She feels rejuvenated, she has more energy, and she feels as though she looks good.

It feels good to be with him because he has lots of energy. Sometimes men over forty start to act old. They have performance issues.

Nowadays many older women like to date younger men for these reasons. Younger men like dating older women because they feel secure, and it reminds them of a maternal relationship. An older woman is usually more experienced sexually, too. Women in their forties, fifties and sixties are active sexually. They enjoy having a younger sex partner.

A woman really enjoys her life during this stage. She is in the prime of her life and often looks more attractive than her younger counterparts. She is active and she takes excellent care of herself. Today she watches her diet and she exercises more than ever. She is energetic and vivacious. She feels good because she is experienced, secure and happy.

There was a man in Taiwan who was twenty years younger than his woman, who was over forty. They were friends to start, and then they started going places together. She felt strange about dating him at first, but after a year or two into the relationship, they each got very comfortable with one another.

He said, "Since you don't want to get married, why don't we live with one another?"

They did, and while they were living together, they started having children together. She had four children by him, all girls. He loved children, but they didn't get married until later in life, after the children were all grown.

They understood each other. They did not have any problems. They were happy together.

Then the couple applied for a visa and passport to come to America, but they had a very hard time getting them. Finally they came to live in the United States. Then they brought their children here. The children made friends easily, but they weren't sure about the food because it tasted so different.

Now they all love it here.

Working With or for a Husband

A wife working for her husband can be in a very precarious position because he can terminate her at any time.

If he fools around with a woman client, she is in an awkward position too. If she says anything, she is likely to be out the door. If she doesn't say anything, she is likely to get an ulcer.

Living Together without Love

A man who has been dating too many women becomes jaded. Either a woman has disappointed him or he has disappointed a woman. Sooner or later women don't mean anything to him because he has been rejected so many times in his life. He also is likely to have been spoiled.

This man is cold, but he still goes after women.

He could actually be a good man because he still longs for intimate contact with a female, but all he has on his mind is that a woman might reject him. He worries about rejection all the time, but he still wants a relationship.

It gives you an empty, sick feeling to come home to someone like this. Even though you have dated him for a long time, he will never say he loves you.

He does not love you. He does not respect you. Instead, he constantly goads you and puts you down.

My Girlfriend Married to My Husband

There was a woman, Cindy, and when she and her husband first broke up, she became hysterical. It was devastating for her. When she then became sick, the husband went out with her girlfriend. That was even more heartbreaking.

After he continued to go out with her friend, she got even more illnesses. She went into a state of shock. She had had four kids to take care of, and he had left her high and dry with them. She sold their big house and bought a small one. She became very angry. She couldn't concentrate. Everything went wrong.

That's what stress does to you. It's a killer. It can ruin your health.

That's why it's so important to focus on you. Do things to maintain your health. Have regular check-ups. Do the things you enjoy. Buy jewelry, and buy the expensive stuff, not the cheap stuff.

Plan activities during times when it would otherwise be difficult for you to be alone. Find things that interest you and that you are good at so you can boost your self-confidence. It's never too late to learn something new. Find out what you like to do. Don't be too hard on yourself.

If you don't have any friends, learn how to entertain yourself. You can volunteer at something you like to do.

Women who Do Not Expect Their Husbands to Ask for a Divorce

There was a woman who found out that her husband wanted a divorce. She hadn't had any idea, but the man had already done all his homework

He had started coming home late, but he said to her that he was busy at work. Then he told her that he was going to take a weeklong business trip without her. After that he stayed at home from time to time, but he didn't want to live there anymore.

He came home late one night and told her that he was going to go on another business trip. He stayed even longer this time.

She had no idea that he actually wanted to stay away from her.

One day after he came back from a long trip, he told her that something was very wrong with him. He told her that he didn't feel like his usual self. He was trying to tell her that he wanted a divorce and that they should spend some time apart so that he could find himself. He was trying to tell her that he was already gone and that he did what he wanted now.

He told her he thought he should move out and find an apartment. He wanted to separate for awhile and see how he felt later. He moved all of his belongings out of the house, and he didn't return home for a while.

She didn't know he was going to drop such a bomb on her.

She felt down and empty. She started to become depressed. She started seeing a psychiatrist because she needed to speak to someone, and no one else would listen to her. She started to take pills and to drink. She was no longer herself.

When you're down so low, you feel as though no one can help you. Everything starts to fall apart.

She had no energy to do anything. She started to feel sorry for herself and she wanted sympathy from her husband. She didn't realize that he was no longer there for her.

In this situation you must find comfort within yourself and regain control of yourself. You can't do crazy things. There is no easy solution to this problem. You have to fix it yourself. No one else can do it for you.

You must stay alert. Don't get wound up. Speak to your lawyer. Do your homework. Focus on your finances. Freeze your assets so he can't wipe you out. Take control of your future. Don't allow his actions to control you and your welfare. Don't allow him to talk you into anything without speaking to your lawyer. Do not sign papers of any kind while you're under the influence of pills or alcohol.

Quit taking the pills. Stop drinking heavily. Concentrate on what you want and what you need. Don't let him talk you into anything.

If he wants a divorce that badly, he will accept whatever you want. Don't settle for less than what you deserve. Ensure your financial security. Ensure that you have what you need to live comfortably throughout your lifetime.

It will be a full-time job to try to settle this divorce. It will take all of your energy and you need to remain focused.

Depending on a Man

There was a woman who lived with a man for seven or eight years. He had kids and she never worked. She forgot about herself.

She was not prepared for what could happen to her. She didn't save any money. She just lived day by day while the man paid all the bills.

One day he threw her out. She had nothing. She had no money. She was totally unprepared.

She had become too comfortable because she didn't have to worry about anything. She never thought their relationship would end this way. She got sick and couldn't do anything. She had no place to live and ended up staying in the YMCA.

When you have problems like this, you would think you could find a friend to help you, but sometimes there is no friend out there. The man wouldn't rescue her because he was looking for someone new.

She became clumsy and she fell all the time. She had to go to the hospital.

She went further into in shock. She finally had to sell all her belongings to get money, and she still couldn't look for a job because she was so sick. She felt sorry for herself and didn't know what to do.

When she left him, she had no money in her pockets, and she did not get enough money to live from selling her belongings either. No one would loan her any money. Sometimes, when it comes to money, even your best friend cannot help you. They have their own problems and they run away from you.

It is hard to correct this situation, but remember, it can be done.

If you are a single woman, you should always work and save your money. Don't touch that money. An emergency will always arise and you will need that money.

Even if you have money, you should still work part-time to discipline yourself and to stay in a routine. Don't tell anyone you are saving this money or they will try to get it from you for some reason. When you're alone, you must be firm with yourself and have self-discipline. Don't always think a man is the answer.

Take care of yourself first before you look for another relationship. You have to be strong for yourself. Get your mind straight. Don't talk about your past with anyone, not even women. They don't want to hear this. They will run away from you.

Once you have had gotten yourself straightened out, you can then start a fresh relationship. When you're in trouble, you must rely upon yourself. Keep busy, so you won't have time to think about your problems.

Don't dwell on your loneliness or feel sorry for yourself. Take long walks, dress up prettily, exercise, and do something to keep yourself busy. Learn how to relax, and try not to sulk because it gives you too much time to dwell on your problems. You must try very hard to straighten yourself out. Don't turn to drugs or alcohol. Try to remember that everyone has a few lonely moments. Just try to keep busy with something productive where you can feel good about yourself.

Pre-nuptials

Pre-nuptials can work for your benefit when they are designed to compensate your for your time if the marriage ends.

Any man who really cares for you will want to share with you. If he doesn't share with you, he's just another person, just another glass of wine. That's it.

. If you live with a man who has money and who has children from a previous marriage, he might want to give his kids everything, not you. He can be afraid of losing the love from his children.

His kids, especially if they're grown, might want all the money, too.

Relatives

Be certain to bring your partner together with all of your relatives, your children and your parents as much as possible. Gather every one together and cook for them or take them out to dinner sometimes.

You should both offer to help your relatives as much as possible, especially if you live close by, with shopping, paying bills, gardening, home maintenance, doctor appointments. This is important. Too many children ignore their parents.

Don't just take your parents for granted. Don't just take their money. Too many children just have their hands out to take the parent's money.

In the Orient, parents train their children much more seriously about life than they do here.

Diminishing Sexual Activity after Marriage

1. Wives begin to remind their husbands of their mothers.

2. Men think of their wives as "good" women who are not fun in bed and who are too sweet and pure and innocent for sex.

3. Women aren't as interested in sex after giving birth because they are preoccupied with raising their children.

4. Men and women expect a decline in interest about sexual activity and accept it without question.

If a relationship is suffering due to tension and arguments, a toll can be taken on the partners. That can negatively effect their sex life.

If a wife has a job outside the home and has kids, too, she has a busy schedule all day and comes home exhausted. When she comes home, she has her other job to take care of her children and her husband. She is exhausted. She goes to bed late in the evening, but she does not fall asleep, she collapses. She doesn't have the faintest interest in sex.

When you are that tired, you can't have sex. You are not there emotionally. Sometimes husbands don't help their wives and the wives come to resent that.

They can harbor ill feelings against the husbands for not cooperating and can subconsciously withhold sex to punish the husbands.

Instead they should work together. The husband should do more than the wife does. That's the way it should be.

This resentment, if allowed to build up, will become worse. The wife's resentment will then be compounded by the husband's resentment. Then the husband is apt to stray.

One day the wife will say, "Why am I doing all this work?" She will be fed up. "Why should I be a slave myself? To keep him? I don't think so."

Some men don't like it if the wife spends too much time with the kids. They start to resent the wife and the kids, too. The man wants the attention she is giving the kids. He is spoiled.

Some men go crazy this way. They go off in the wrong direction and sometimes never come back. The wife can then try to keep her husband on a short leash and pull him back in if she can. Sometimes, however, the husband will resist and make her task and her life impossible.

A man like this doesn't think. He just does.

Female who is not Responsive

Women do not always have an orgasm, even though they may have attained a high level of arousal during the excitement and the plateau stages. There can be a number of reasons for this. A woman can be more easily distracted by her thoughts or by concerns at these stages than a man, for instance.

Some women may not reach an orgasm at all during their lovemaking or during a particular episode of sexual activity. This does not necessarily detract from the pleasure they have experienced during the other stages of intercourse, however, and they may feel sexually fulfilled just the same.

Unfaithfulness

When a partner is betrayed due to the other's unfaithfulness, it is perceived as not only a violation of the sexual aspect of the relationship, but also as a deep betrayal from a psychological standpoint. When the infidelity is discovered, it shakes the very foundation of the relationship. Sometimes, like Humpty Dumpty's egg, things are beyond repair.

The injured relationship hobbles along and the couple may grudgingly stay together out of familiarity and convenience, but their joy and love, in the purest sense, will probably never be the same. They just "go through the motions."

This is not to discourage couples from going for counseling and trying to mend their fences. Any efforts taken in that direction are commendable. But couples should be prepared for the worst case scenario, a failure to resolve the problem.

Here is a story to illustrate the devastating effects this situation can have.

After being married for ten years to a wonderful husband, a wife meets a man, a complete stranger, on the Internet.

Much later on she tries to re-capture her relationship with her husband, but she realizes that the marriage was already over and beyond any repair when she met the man on the Internet. She sees their relationship was actually a confused and frustrated, childless ten years of marriage.

This couple has continued to have problems when Mrs. X, who is around forty, somewhat overweight, bored and frustrated, starts writing to a man in a chat room on the Internet. She lives in southern Connecticut and he lives in a remote town in South Carolina.

The attraction is because of loneliness on her part and on his part, too. In addition, he was searching for a maternal image and for someone to provide a means of financial support for himself.

After communicating via the chat room for some time, the two decide to meet. She drove down to South Carolina and the physical affair began. Their affair is torrid, and is what she believes at the time to be "true love." It continues for a year and a half.

Then her husband meets a young, beautiful woman and begins a relationship with her. This triggers jealousy within the wife.

Simultaneously, her Internet lover has become much less appealing. The novelty has worn off, and so has the sexual attraction between the two of them. He hasn't worked since the inception of the affair. She has become tired of eating Chinese take out and renting a three dollar video when she goes to visit him. She now hates hearing him laugh out loud at things she used to think were funny. It is over. She knows it.

She wants her husband back. She asks him to go away for a weekend together to try to re-kindle the relationship.

He agrees, but he has to tell his girlfriend he is going away with his wife to try to patch things up. This puts a slight wrench in that relationship. That's just what his wife wanted, of course.

The weekend turns out to be a disaster. They both realize the marriage is over.

The husband divorces the wife and reconciles with his girlfriend. He did do what any good husband would do in an attempt to save the marriage. She can't hold that against him for too long.

So the moral of this story is: Before you decide to cheat on your spouse, you better be prepared for the consequences. This goes for men or women.

Men who Lack Responsibility

A woman should not take a man in who does not do his share of the workload.

Little does a woman know that sometimes a man is basically living there rent free and socking his money away. In several years, he is able to leave because he has saved up enough. Now he can go take up with someone else.

Here's an example of a man who lacks responsibility. A husband agreed to have lunch with his wife, but then, at the very last minute, decided to do something else instead. Although he had made the plans with her to go to lunch, he decided instead to go play golf with his son from his first marriage. This gave the wife the signal that he really did not care about her.

The good feelings between them gradually eroded as one thing after another occurred like this. The wife, although not the jealous sort, became resentful of the preferential treatment by her husband toward his son. When she tries to speak to the husband about it, the husband acts cavalier and demonstrates his "so what?" attitude. This is painful for her and eventually leads to weakening their relationship.

Mixed Signals

Communicating with mixed signals is the perfect way to drive your partner absolutely crazy. When you give a person the signal for yes and then act in a way that emphatically says no, you can drive the other person up the wall.

Husbands and wives must learn to understand each other. The mixed messages that either one can receive can have a dangerous effect on them, even though they otherwise cherish each other.

A mixed message may not be mean spirited behavior.

It usually begins when we don't say what we want to say. The underlying cause is a reluctance to express what we feel, think, or expect. We fear that honest communication may damage the relationship.

A vicious cycle can begin. These crazy-making messages bring on similar responses. Tension increases. Trust is destroyed. Sexual compatibility can deteriorate in what had been an intimate relationship.

It is ironic that mixed messages arise most often in relationships that we genuinely value.

Eliminate mixed messages by understanding your own feelings. Don't worry about psychoanalyzing the other person.

For example, a man keeps saying that he's going to take you to a show or to dinner, but he always has an excuse as to why he cannot go. Or your husband says to you that he will go on vacation, but he suddenly doesn't feel like going or he refuses to make any plans with you for the vacation.

Then you have to make plans to go by yourself or with your friends.

Compliments/Caring

A man has to learn how to compliment a woman on the way she looks, on her hair, her clothing, her make-up, her company, or her choice in restaurant. He has to compliment her on something. He has to show interest in her in order to make her happy and nourish the relationship. Otherwise, she is going to feel like she is just there.

If a man loves you, he will want to take you everywhere he goes.

When you first meet a man, you are so excited, but don't get too excited. It's not worth it. Calm down. Relax.

A woman, even though she is married, must take care of herself. She still has to watch her clothes and her weight. She must exercise and have facial care.

Married to a Jealous Man

Every time you go out of the house, a jealous man times you. He asks you when you will be home.

When you return, he asks, "Where did you go? What did you do?"

Even when you are on the phone, he is jealous. He stands there and listens.

He goes into your purse and looks for phone numbers. If he sees a suspicious phone number, he will call that person. Sometimes when you go out, he follows you.

Sometimes he will call you pretending to be another man. Tell him, "You have the wrong phone number." If he calls back, as he sometimes will, do the same thing.

A woman can be jealous sometimes. When her husband is with her, he shouldn't stare at another woman. It's embarrassing and it makes his wife feel like nothing. She will lose her affection for him, and it can eventually destroy a relationship. She begins to say to herself, "Why am I with him?" It begins to bother her all the time. She feels like she can't trust him. She thinks he's acting like he is in a jungle and has never seen a woman before.

When a man goes out with his wife or girlfriend, he should not stare at other women or his partner's feelings will change toward him. She can get cold over something as stupid as that. When a man is with woman, he has to make her feel special.

Jealousy thrives where there is insecurity. Jealousy is dangerous. It can not only cause trouble and very bad arguments, but it can even lead to violence.

However, a very small amount of jealousy can perk up a relationship. It keeps both people alert to the special qualities in the other.

Make Time for Your Husband

When you are in a relationship, be certain not to take the other person for granted.

Make time for him or her.

Do the things your husband likes, at least some of the time. Take drives in the country together. Do simple things together. Read the New York Times together. Do the crossword together. Go bicycling together. Go to the beach. Take time to be together after work.

Make sure you watch for those warning signals that your partner might be restless or might have unfulfilled dreams.

If you don't do those things with him, he might find someone else who will.

Wives who Put Their Husbands Through School

There was a couple who got married, but the husband did not have a good profession.

His wife said to him, "Why don't you go to school and get your education?"

So he went to school and she worked hard outside the home and took care of the house and the children. She even started a new business for him.

He became very successful and started making a lot of money.

When he traveled, he took his secretary with him. She started accompanying him even when they went on family vacations. The wife did not realize that the secretary was after her husband.

Pretty soon, their marriage fell apart. They stopped communicating and they didn't do things together anymore. They separated.

He married the secretary and the two of them lived together happily.

His children had grown up, and the wife now lived alone in the big house.

As long as she lived, she never trusted another man. She had worked hard to help him make it, and then he left with a younger woman.

She thought her life was done, but it wasn't. Her problem was that she thought that it was.

She should have learned how to live in the present and the future, not in the past.

Her life could have been new and fresh.

She should have taken time for herself. Listened to music. Learned how to laugh and have fun again. She should have joined clubs. Made new friends. She needed to learn how to be happy again, not sad and depressed.

When you're down and sad, play happy music, not sad music, because sad music will really make you cry.

If you have been dumped by someone, the pain will be different than if you have lost someone who has passed away. In either case, though, you need to retain your focus.

There isn't any medicine for the pain, either. You just need to get back into your routine. Remember the good times. Let them stay with you. You must have some beautiful memories of times with that person which will always stay with you. No one can ever take those memories away. They belong to you forever, no matter what.

Don't wallow in the pain any more than you have to, but sometimes, briefly, you do have to wallow in the pain because that's human nature. It is a natural reaction and a grieving process after we have suffered tremendous loss.

If you believe in God, pray. Sooner or later, God will hear you and He will answer your prayers. You must keep the faith.

Married to a Handsome Man

A handsome man prefers a woman who is not gorgeous.

He may not always be looking for a woman, but they are always after him. If a woman makes a proposition, however, he is not apt to refuse.

There are many women who would go after someone else's handsome husband. A wife has to work hard to keep that man around. A wife always has to be looking out for what can happen to him.

Women easily pick up on the fact that a man is loose. If he is handsome and has money, watch out. It will be hard to keep him with you, especially if he does not value marriage or women highly. It's a full time job to watch him. Usually you can tell by looking at a man, the expression on a man's face and his mannerisms what he is thinking about and what he has been up to.

If he laughs too much, it could mean that he's genuinely happy, but it can also mean he's up to no good. Some men are easily brainwashed by other women, especially if they have a problem at home or are a little bored or if they have started to lose interest in their wives. Other women can easily manipulate them if they are weakened in this way.

If a wife cares for her husband and does not want to lose him to another woman, she can object loudly; but this can compound the problem because her husband can get rebellious and decide to teach her a lesson.

Husband who Travels

When a man goes on vacation separately from you, he either does not want to spend money on you or he has somebody else there.

Secretary/Younger Woman

Be careful of other women who are only drawn to men who are taken, but seem available. Beware of men who travel more than usual, who start coming home late more often, who become distant, who spend more money on themselves. You might have to have them followed.

In one way, men and women are very different. Men have a strong sexual appetite, whereas most women's sex drive is lower. Men can be compulsive this way.

One night a husband and wife and her girlfriend went out together. The husband and girlfriend went back to the car and started messing around. Later the husband divorced his wife, even though they had three children, and married her girlfriend. The wife became hysterical and developed bleeding ulcers, cancer and thyroid problems. She later married an older man, but he died.

You have to get involved in your husband's business.

One husband went out with his secretary. He said he "had to marry her so she would not be an old maid." When he divorced his wife, she ended up with almost no money. Some men are like little children. If you don't pay attention to them, they are gone. You have to treat them like little kids.

Some men do not know how to take care of a woman so they end up looking for someone else. Other men, who have gotten married too young, eventually get divorced because of their egos. They want to start again because they feel like they are missing something. In both cases, if their children have grown up, the women are left "lost souls." Usually those men will wait until their children are eighteen before they leave.

Men, not matter how old they are, can always get married to another woman. Women can't do that. They suffer. Only if a woman is young can she start over.

Pregnancy

First you say, "I'm going to have a baby."

In two months, you should be pregnant and happy.

Talk to your husband and your friends and your mother-in-law while you carry the baby.

Don't worry, don't be depressed, and don't be unhappy because whatever you do goes with both you and your baby. If you feel pressured, then the child also feels what you feel.

If you want to have a healthy and happy baby, avoid alcohol, caffeine, salt, meat, and drugs. Only take what the doctor prescribes. Get an exercise plan from your doctor which you can safely do.

You could develop your own program and routine, too, if it's safe.

Successful Marriage

A strong man doesn't complain. He can handle any problems that come into his hands.

Don't keep telling him things over and over again. You can tell him once and he won't forget. He's independent. He can do for himself, as he is very capable.

This man will do lots for you. Whatever you ask for, he will provide.

You must do your part. If he comes home from work, you must have everything prepared. He's hungry. He likes to eat. When he comes, he does not want to hear any problems. Don't talk about unpleasant things before or during dinner. Try to handle things yourself. The only thing you might want to discuss is a little emergency.

Make sure his clothes are always ready for him. Wash them and iron them and have them dry cleaned as necessary.

Don't complicate things with him too much. He doesn't like things to be too complex. He like things to be streamlined.

He will give you all of his paycheck and let you pay the bills. Be careful with what you do with the money. Spend wisely. If you want to spend more than $250.00 on yourself, then you better discuss it with him. Tell him where the money goes.

Keep every receipt. File your bills and receipts carefully, in order by date. You can keep them in a book titled "monthly expenses." Mark down the date when you paid the bill and write down the checking account and the check number. If you pay the bills by phone, get a confirmation number or the name of the person you spoke with, and mark down the date and how much you paid in your book.

Then he will feel comfortable.

If he's very busy, then help him with his business. It will make him feel good. He needs to feel important. Even though he has employees, you should still help him with some of the work, either the confidential matters or some other area of your choosing.

Make sure you save some money because you never know when a rainy day is going to come around unexpectedly. This is especially true if you only have one paycheck coming in.

Try not to throw out old clothes. Try to find ways to re-design old clothes because good fabric can last a long time. If you re-design them, you can have a current or a new look at no cost to you except for the time it takes to sew. You can take sewing courses at home, by mail or on line.

That way you can stay home with the kids.

Unconsummated Marriages

As difficult as it is to believe, it is true that eight per cent of married couples have never had sexual intercourse.

The reason could be one of many: over-attachment to family; strict backgrounds; physical disabilities; impotence; sexually transmitted diseases. In these instances, it is advisable for the couple to obtain professional counseling on the underlying cause.

A Husband with Baggage

When a husband has been married before and has children from a previous marriage, he must be careful not to undermine the present marriage by boasting constantly about his children or his ex-wife to either his current wife or to other people. It will tend to make her feel unimportant, small, and unloved.

While she can tolerate this for a while, it will inevitably wear her down and make her feel resentful. She cannot feel good about herself. She will think it is her fault that he is obsessing about his former family. She will try other things to please him, hoping that he will no longer obsess about them, but when that fails, she will become despondent about their relationship.

If an ex-wife or his children control a man, then you have to leave. It will never change, especially if this man's words don't match his actions. Talk is cheap.

There was a man who had been married three times. He had two grown children from his first marriage. He spent an inordinate amount of time with these children, to the point of the exclusion of his third wife. Especially hurtful to the third wife was being kept away from many holiday celebrations. When she was included, however, the children maligned her and put her down. The husband said nothing. When she brought it to his attention later on, he pretended that he had not heard anything.

CHAPTER V
FINANCES DURING
MARRIAGE

Credit Cards/Bank Accounts

Even if the two of you have a joint credit card, it is better that you also have your own credit card in your own name. You must make sure that your credit card is being paid on time, if you are not the one paying the bills, in order to keep your credit squeaky-clean. If you borrow money from a bank, those bills must be paid on time, too. It is very important to keep your credit clean or up to date, especially if you have children.

It's also very important to have your husband put the necessary funding in your name. Don't let him just talk about it. Make him do it. If he doesn't, give him an ultimatum. If he wants to keep you, he will do it. You don't want to be stuck up any financial creek without a paddle.

By doing these things, somewhere down the road, if your husband decides to leave you and run off with his secretary, you would be protected. You will have security, especially if there are children involved. You do need to protect not only yourself, but your children as well.

Some men, as they get older, become strange. They might decide to take a trip around the world, without you, in search of themselves. Where would you be at that point?

There is a reason why these things are important. The next stories are prime examples.

There was a woman who one day went to her bank and wanted to withdraw money. The bank told her that she was no longer a customer there. There was no money left in the account. She went to use her credit card, but she could no longer use the card because her husband had canceled it, too.

She had to walk around with no money in her pocket. She could not go shopping for groceries or anything. He had suddenly wiped her out of everything.

There was another husband who told his wife that he had to go off to find himself. This was not really true. He went off to be with another woman. This man had done his homework with this other woman for about ten years before his wife ever found out he had a girlfriend.

His wife went crazy. Now she takes Prozac. She can hardly talk. She is in la-la land.

It is going to be very difficult for her now to ever change her mind and get over it.

Only you can change your own mind. No one else. Make sure you know what you are doing.

A man can try to take advantage of you. He can even say you are crazy and try to work that against you.

There was another woman who could do everything. She did the gardening, sewed the curtains, cleaned, shopped. She did it all. She went away twice a year on a vacation paid for by her husband. This was ideal.

Wife More Financially Secure than Husband

There was a woman who was married with children. She was an executive in a large company, but her husband was not a good provider. She managed to take care of the children and the house without his help.

Her parents had always told her to make certain she had a good education and a good job, even though she might be married. She listened to her parents. She provided a very good home for her children and she had somebody to help take care of them.

She finally got divorced from the first husband because he was not a good provider. She paid the bills and he did not.

She married again, and her second marriage was good. Her second husband made good money, but she continued to work so that she could have security in her life and so that she could send her children to a good school. In case she ever ran into problems later on, she would have her own money. She led a better life this way. Now she even makes more money than her second husband.

Sometimes work helps you and you don't worry so much. When you don't worry, you automatically feel healthier and happier. That's the way to live.

This couple invested money together by buying real estate. They put both their names on the properties. They didn't use the same lawyer. They always protected themselves. They each had their own savings account with no one else's name on it.

A husband shouldn't think he doesn't have to work so hard if his wife makes more money than he does.

Don't take a vacation too often, but if you take a vacation, you must go together. If he wants to go alone once in a while, that's okay, but if he does this too often, you are in trouble.

A husband has to do a lot of work around the house for his family. He cannot go outside the home and do things for others. Otherwise trouble arises. A husband should ask a wife what projects he should do, what errands he should run, what things he should do around the house. He should see if there is shopping he can do or if she needs help with the bills. A husband has to ask his wife what he can do for her. A couple needs a lot of communication.

Finances

You have to concentrate on your finances during marriage.

Don't think you are necessarily going to be married forever. The divorce rate statistics are over fifty percent against you. This means that you have to plan ahead for any consequences. This does not mean that you should be pessimistic, only realistic. You should plan for your future "just in case" disaster strikes.

It could happen to you, no matter how much in love with your husband you think you are, and no matter how good things are. If he really loves you, he will understand and he will help you secure a nest egg that is all your own. That will prove to you that he loves you and will give you peace of mind. This is important.

If you never pay the bills during the marriage, it will be difficult for you to learn about them all of a sudden. It is recommended that you learn how to do your own finances while you are married. Set aside time once a week in the evening or on the weekend when you are alone. Fill out the yearly income sheets that follow last year's income tax return form. You should have all the information you need about your income.

Some men don't want you to learn anything about the finances. This is another method of control. When you do learn, though, and the man leaves or dies, you can relax and move on with your life gracefully. You will be secure and happy that you had learned earlier. You will be proud of yourself, too, that you can be so comfortable. You will be stress free.

To start learning, gather last year's checks and monthly bank statements. Sort the checks and monthly bank statements according to categories. Break down your credit card expenses by category and add the total to the subtotal on the yearly expense sheet. You should use separate cards for your business and personal expenses to make record keeping easier. You may also save money by tracking credit card interest for business expenses. Interest for business expenses is tax deductible.

You probably also wrote a few checks for cash, and you may have withdrawn cash from a bank machine. Look at your bank statements to find those amounts. Add up the total and insert under "miscellaneous cash."

Know how much you spend each month. Sometimes people don't want to know how much they spend, but you must know even if it is unpleasant. Women need to know all of these things. Sometimes we choose to be oblivious to our finances.

Compare this to visiting your doctor for a mammogram. You are afraid to go, but you know you need to go for your own good. You put it off, but it is inevitable that you must go. You don't want to be like an ostrich that puts its head in the sand.

If you eventually want some luxuries—new clothing, new shoes, a manicure or a pedicure—you must budget yourself accordingly.

The basic rule of thumb is "if you don't have it, don't spend it."

Although you always need clothes and shoes, for example, you're never going to get the money back that you spend for those items. Of course, if you learn to be a smart shopper, as many women are learning to do today, you will shop at the consignment shops and seek out the ones that have the quality you want. There are some very high end consignment shops which have clothing and shoes that have never been worn or that have only been worn gently.

If a person consigns clothing to a consignment store, the store will typically price an item at one quarter of the original value. The store generally gives a 50/50 split, which yields the consignor approximately 12 ½ % of the original value. Stop and think about that before you spend money on brand new clothes or shoes.

Before you charge on your charge card, make sure that it is in your budget. Know how much you can spend each month without getting your head in a noose.

Home expenses can be tax deductible if, for example, they pertain to home improvement. If you own your home, there are also some things you can depreciate on the house. Look into the federal tax books to learn more about this or ask your accountant. Learn how to write off as many expenses as you can. The federal government affords you this so take advantage of the savings.

You should always keep canceled checks and file them. Sometimes you might be billed twice, and you don't want to have to pay twice. So keep your bills in order.

Be careful that you do not shop while you are under stress. You will be apt to buy things you don't need or can't use. Don't be a compulsive shopper.

There were a man and a woman who married even though they didn't know each other well. They had joint checking and saving accounts. He worked every day and she trusted her husband.

One day he took all their savings and he charged all their credit cards to the maximum.

It took the wife five years to pay off his bills, and there were no children for her to support. She says she'll never trust a man again.

One man like that spoils it for the rest of men. He went through everything they had because he just wanted to have a good time on her money. It's a real learning experience.

Be careful. Never give just any man your credit card or your information for a bank account. You have to watch your money.

CHAPTER VI
ENDING A RELATIONSHIP

Marriage is no Guarantee

What do you do when you are hit with an unexpected divorce?

You don't know if you should go to a bar or start hitting the bottle at home. Your friends are just as shocked as you are. You start crying. You start to smoke a lot. You drink more. You have a great deal of difficulty concentrating. You have trouble getting up in the morning because you are depressed. You start to call in sick to work.

Your life is a disaster. You used to do your job perfectly, but not any longer. Everything you touch seems to go wrong for some unexplained reason and due to no fault of your own.

Don't feel self-conscious. You are not a bad person. You are a good person with bad things happening to you.

This creates loneliness. You could get married again, but that might be good or might bad for you now. You could get married to someone you don't love, for instance. After you go through a tragedy, be very careful.

You may be anesthetizing yourself with medications and alcohol and not thinking very clearly. In everything you do, you seem to make mistakes. You are so wound up that you can't concentrate. You feel like you are going crazy. Sometimes you make mistakes on important things because you are so confused.

Sooner or later, if you're not careful, you will have trouble retaining any employment. Your friends, where are they? Everyone you turn to rejects you. They no longer want to hear your problems.

You are the only one who ultimately can cope with this kind of problem. If you want to work on it, it takes a while to correct all the problems that you have accumulated. Sometimes you don't know where to start. You are overwhelmed with everything.

Even your body is so confused that you cannot function correctly. You used to exercise daily. Now you are too depressed to exercise. When you are under stress, sometimes your blood pressure is very high and you have trouble breathing. You can develop migraine headaches.

Whatever you do, make sure you relax and put your feet up. Watch a pleasant movie or listen to soft music.

If you can't sleep, this is very harmful for your body. You should cut down on your medication and any drinking. Moderation is key.

Don't completely cut out all your activities, but give yourself some time to heal. Don't be too hard on yourself.

Sometimes you can gain weight or sometimes you might get too thin, depending on your thyroid glands. If you are gaining or losing weight, you might seek the advice of a trusted physician.

You need to find someone you can trust, too, someone you can talk to a little bit without fear of recrimination.

There was a woman who never expected to get divorced from her husband.

She had first met this man in college. He would help her with her homework. They dated for two years and became very attracted to each other.

They were from different cultures. She was Italian, but she was born in the United States. His family was from Greece. During their college years, her mother would make her come home from school every time she tried to get together with him for a while. Her parents did not approve of him. Automatically they had not liked him.

The couple had an extremely difficult time getting together because of the interference from her parents. Finally she arranged a vacation to go with him to Hawaii, but her mother would not let her go. She told her daughter to go and stay at home. Every time she tried to take a trip somewhere, her mother interfered. She was not allowed to make any plans by herself.

After they graduated, they both moved back to their homes. Her mother had told her to come home and rest before she got a job. When she got home, she told her parents more about her boyfriend. She told her parents that he was very bright and that he used to help her do her homework in college. Every time she asked this man difficult questions, she said, he would come up with the answers right away because he was very smart.

The two wrote to each other; however, her mother intercepted the letters. They had a hard time communicating. Her mother told her daughter that when she started working, she would have to go non-stop and she would never see him.

She invited him to her house to meet her parents because she had become so serious about him, and he about her. They were very much in love and wanted to get married. He came to visit, and her mother told her not to marry this man.

She told her daughter that he might be a very nice guy, but that something about him just was not right. She told her he was not the man for her.

Her mother was so strict that she ran away from home. She took a year and looked for a job in New York.

She was in love with this man and felt she had to be with him. They both got jobs in New York and he went to live there. It took them several years to get married because of her parents, but they finally had a very small marriage ceremony in New York.

After they had been married for three years, they decided to move to Greenwich so they could raise the children there. They got along very well. They never fought. They did everything together.

After they had children, the husband got promoted. He took on a very responsible position and traveled all over the world. She raised the children.

He took many, many trips, but if he said he would be home, he would be home on time. If he said he wanted to spend time with the children, he would do it. While the children were in school, he didn't take any vacations so he could be home for them. He was always home on weekends.

She always thought he was a good husband. She thought he was loyal to the children and to her. Every time he was away, he would call every other day. They remained very much in love with each other and felt as if they were still on their honeymoon together.

After a twenty-eight year marriage, she thought he was the best father in the world for the children. She was completely relaxed with him after all those years. He was always smiling and laughing and was always good-natured with the children.

Then, one time, he went away on business. He called her from the airport and told her he had missed his plane. She didn't pay too much attention because this had happened before.

But this time he didn't come home for a week.

He stopped spending time with the children. He would just give them his credit card.

The family had an apartment in New York and one day she told him that she wanted to bring the children into New York. She said the four of them could go out to a fancy dinner.

He told her that he just wanted to be alone.

One night he came home late and slept in the guestroom. She heard him, but she pretended she was asleep.

She got up the next morning and made coffee and breakfast for the two of them. He told her that he had not come to her room because he had come home so late and had not wanted to wake her up.

As usual she drove him to the train station so he could get to work in New York. They didn't talk on the way. As he got out of the car, he told her that he would call her later.

When he called, he told her that she shouldn't wait with dinner for him.

She still thought nothing of it. She didn't think anything was wrong.

She told him on the phone that one of the children was going to have a birthday party that weekend and asked him if he could send out invitations to their friends. He told her that he wasn't coming home that night. He was staying in New York.

The next day he went to Europe.

The party took place without him. He left an envelope with money in it for the child's birthday. Everyone at the party asked her where he was. She told everyone that he was in Europe, but she was finally starting to get suspicious.

She didn't have any idea, though, that her husband might want a divorce, even though they had not slept in the same bed for five months.

He started regularly coming home late. He wasn't home much at all anymore. He told her that he was busy at work. He took another business trip for a week without her.

He came home late one night and told her that he was going on another business trip. He stayed away even longer this time.

Two weeks later, he came back and went to their New York apartment. He called her from there and told her that he had just arrived that night. He said that he felt tired and had a cold and a sore throat.

The next day he told her he had to go to the doctor. The day after that he said he could not get rid of the cold. He didn't come home until a week later.

By this time, she knew that something was very wrong. She cried herself to sleep at night.

The children would ask her what was wrong. Her son thought his father was having an affair and he asked his mother if she wanted him to follow his father. She told him, "Not yet."

He finally came home a week later.

She told him that she had invited a lot of friends over on Sunday and was expecting about sixty people.

On Saturday, she told him that she wanted to talk with him. She said that she knew something was wrong because he had not been home very much lately, and he always had been home a lot. She told him that he seemed confused and that he was not the same man she was married to before. Something was not right. She said that she felt he didn't want to be with her anymore.

Her husband told her that something had happened to him and that he had been thinking all of this time. He told her that he just wanted to be by himself for a while.

In reality, he had another woman.

One day, after he had come back from a long trip, he told her again that something was very wrong with him. He didn't feel like his usual self.

He wanted to tell her that he wanted a divorce and that he was already gone from their marriage. Instead he said that maybe they should spend some time apart so that he could find himself. He told her that he needed to move out and find an apartment. He wanted to be by himself.

She had never dreamed that he would say these things to her. She couldn't talk. She just went to her bedroom and cried like a baby. She had always felt that this man had been sincere, that he had loved her. Now she couldn't believe it.

She felt like the man she had loved had been dead for the past two years.

He moved all of his belongings out and left her in their big house by herself.

He told her that financially she did not have to worry. The children had all grown up, had graduated from college and had moved away from home. He told her that if there was anything she needed or wanted, or that if she needed to talk to him, she should get in touch with him.

She didn't know what to do.

She called her girlfriend and explained to her what had happened. She was crying so much that her girlfriend could hardly understand her.

Her girlfriend came to her house to comfort her and told her that when men are very successful and make a lot of money, they do crazy things. They think they are missing something and they start all over again.

She told her girlfriend that she couldn't keep the house because it was too big. Her girlfriend said that she assumed her husband would want part of the house anyway, but that she was lucky in a way, because she would at least be comfortable.

Much later she told her girlfriend that she had never told her this, but that she was going to tell her now. When her husband had left, he had run away with her other girlfriend.

She had been married for twenty years and had three children. There were two mortgages on the house. The wife had gone to the bank to withdraw money, but he had taken all of the money from the bank. She didn't have enough money to pay the bills, and her mother had to help her get by. She sold the house, but barely had enough money to pay off the mortgage. She told her girlfriend all this, too.

She ended up in the hospital many times. No one could help her. She told her girlfriend that she had been sick for years and years and that she didn't think she would ever get over it. She did not understand how he could have done those things to her. She had brought his children into the world and hadn't worked outside the home. She had taken care of everybody.

She told her girlfriend that she had entertained many people at their home almost every week, but after she got sick, no one called. No one came over. All she had left were her three children.

She had raised her children by herself and they had all grown up, were working and had been successful. They took care of their mother now. They watched over her. They helped her keep the house.

She told her girlfriend that her children were wonderful to her and that she was very lucky. She said this had been going on for four years, but that she didn't think she would ever get over it. She used to be so healthy and now everything was wrong with her because of her ex-husband.

Her girlfriend told her that she had to learn to be strong and had to start all over again. She told her that she had to find help. She needed someone to talk to. She told her not to talk to her other friends, who had deserted her, but she could talk to her. She might need to talk to a professional, too. She told her not to let herself go. He wasn't worth getting sick over. She suggested she take a trip, maybe with her children, and told her she shouldn't stay in the house all the time.

The woman felt empty and depressed. She started seeing a psychiatrist. She needed to speak to someone, and she felt she needed professional help. She was stuck on the idea that she was still in love with him, despite all

She had moved into a very small house by herself. She started to take pills and to drink. She was no longer herself. She was down so low she had gone into a state of shock. Sometimes she didn't even know what she was talking about. Everything started to fall apart, and she had no energy to do anything.

She started to feel sorry for herself. She still wanted sympathy from her husband.

She had to realize that he was no longer there for her and that she must find comfort within herself. She had to regain control of herself.

When this situation happens to you, you can't do crazy things. There are no easy solutions. You have to start all over again. No one else can do it for you.

You must stay alert and not get wound up. You have to speak to your lawyer, do your homework, focus on your finances, and, if necessary, freeze your assets so he can't wipe you out. You must take control of your future and not allow his actions to control you or your welfare.

Do it Yourself Divorce

If you are getting a divorce and you and your husband don't have many assets, you would likely benefit from either mediation or the do-it-yourself divorce kit that is readily available at a book store or law library. The state may also provide assistance for you if you qualify.

Difficult Break-up

If you love someone, you are going to remember him for a long time.

If you love someone, it is therefore difficult to re-program your mind about that person. However, it can be done successfully with a focused level of concentration. Otherwise, you will always be living in the past, not in the present or the future.

Train yourself to forget that person. It can be done. Sometimes you may have trouble forgetting him until you find someone else to replace him. You may be sad and you may cry until that happens, but it's only natural to feel a sense of loss and to mourn that loss. You can have trouble getting him off your mind because of the memories you shared. If someone tells you to forget him, it is still difficult. People around you should understand this.

Know Who You Are

Before you can truly develop a relationship with a man, you need to know yourself. You need to be honest about what you really want for yourself in life.

Creating a strong self-esteem and developing a good relationship with yourself builds a solid foundation from which you can open yourself up to a relationship with a man. This is very important to do and will help you to be successful in your relationship.

The first place to begin is with your body. Its health and vitality will give you the fitness and energy to enjoy your own life and to commit yourself with enthusiasm to another person. Simple steps can be taken at first to enhance your life. A change to a healthy diet will give you the right balance of nutrition. You'll feel good and you'll look good. A regular program of exercise—stretching, walking or aerobic workouts—will keep your muscles toned and your cardiovascular system in good condition.

Certain exercises are designed to deepen your breathing and to release blocked emotional feelings. Through them you can feel a greater sense of freedom and spontaneity.

You can take good care of your skin and your muscle tone by using self-massage.

This technique will help you feel relaxed and invigorated.

A self-awareness program will make you feel positive about yourself and draw others to you.

__Attitude__

It is very important that you have a good attitude.

Cast off negativity. Turn negatives into positives. There are so many people you come in contact with who have negative attitudes. Be careful because these can be absorbed by you and internalized. Don't get angry by others' negative attitudes, but shake them off right away. Those people are unhappy and they want to bring you down too.

Don't be down. Be upbeat. Find something positive in everything you do.

Even though this is rather a cliché, it is true. When you are sad, make yourself happy. Try to find something to laugh at. When you laugh, the whole world does seem to laugh with you, but remember that when you cry, you cry alone.

First, confront yourself. Why are you lonely? Did you just lose someone through divorce or death or a break-up? Was it sudden or was it expected?

If it was expected, it is hard enough; but if it is sudden, the results can be devastating. There is no medicine for this condition. You can find it very difficult to concentrate. You can't function. You are confused, bewildered, and depressed.

It is as if you were a deer and, blinded by the headlights of a car, you got hit in the middle of the night. You say to yourself, "What just happened?"

Most of your friends vanish because they don't have the time or the desire to help you deal with your problems. Life becomes painful for you and frustrating. You did not expect this tragedy to happen.

You must get through it and you will. It just takes time. No one can say just how much time it will take you to heal your wounds.

You may not ever completely heal. But it can get better, and it will.

The more you get back into your routine, the better off you will feel. Remember to do the things you loved the most before the tragedy occurred. It is very important that you do the things you enjoy doing. These will help.

Keep busy. Develop new projects. Try to find things to do where you can work with your hands. This is therapeutic and becomes a sort of therapy through which you can release your unhappiness.

Do things with your friends. Get out with other people. Make a list of things you want to do.

You have to have a plan. Make a list of short term goals. Make a list of long term goals. These will help you focus.

Don't hang around with those so-called "friends" who put you down and make you miserable. They will not help you get better. Don't keep company with those friends who are arrogant and only tell you to "get on with your life." They are not sensitive to your needs.

This is a time to "clean house," even though to do this can be painful. These people are not really your friends. They are looking to see you go down. Rid these people from your life. Don't bother with them anymore.

They are insulting you by making you feel worse. Some people are just sinister and jealous and have no compassion. They can feel superior if they see you have problems. This is because they really have inferiority complexes. They were jealous of your life as it was. Now they have the chance to stick it to you.

If you really have no one worth talking to, then talk to yourself.

Sometimes you do need alone time, but not too much. Only talk with those people who give you solace and understanding. Perhaps they have been through something similar. Go on dates or go out with good friends.

You need to work on yourself and on healing yourself.

Don't let anybody know what happened except a few select friends whom you can trust.

Don't torture yourself if there was a break up. He probably already did enough of that to you without you getting down on yourself as well.

Your life is not done. You can get over this. Anytime you see anyone you know, including your ex, just smile and be pleasant.

When it is appropriate to laugh, then feel free to do so. Give yourself permission to enjoy life again.

When you are younger, it's easier. When you are older, although it is slightly more difficult, you can still have a new and even a better life than you had before. If you clean up what's bothering you, you will be a new person again.

It can be good to get involved in meditation.

If your mind starts to think about things that are sad or depressing, just think about funny things that you have done in the past. Then you will laugh. Put some nice thing in your mind.

Positive emotions are based around smiling. You have to discipline yourself at first to smile. Remember that. Smiles help you live longer.

Do something you like to do every day. You could draw or do some other kind of artwork, for instance.

Don't be by yourself all of the time. Don't take a vacation until you get all of this straightened up with your ex. Don't stay wound up. Don't try to make your ex feel sorry for you. Chances are that he's not going to come back.

The chances that he will come back are, however, increased if you were a married couple who had children together because you have that very special bond through your children that continues on.

When you are sad, be aware that many of your so called friends will run away from you.

In life, when you have a difficult time, you have to learn how to get through things. Even though you are sad, not everything is bad. Life has to be full of ups and downs. That way you can learn how to get through anything.

When you do get through, you can teach other people how to make their lives better. In other countries, people know how to laugh and to be happy despite the ups and downs. In this country, there is too much unhappiness. Maybe we don't know how to laugh and be happy. Maybe we are pre-programmed to be unhappy here.

After you survive this turmoil, you will be the strongest person you have ever been in your entire life, so don't let this problem beat you. You need to resign yourself to beating the problem. This is easier said, of course, than done; but it can be done. Worry and frustrations take a toll on you. Don't let them drain you completely.

You might want to consider getting a dog, a cat, or another animal for company. They are nice to come home to and will give you unconditional affection.

Watch the colors you wear and the ones you have in your home. Don't wear or decorate with too much white. Don't wear too much black by itself. If you have to wear black, mix it with other colors.

Validation

Remember that it is important to validate your true feelings.

Your feelings are real. You are entitled to them. Own your feelings. Don't let anyone tell you that you are not entitled to own your feelings. This is very important.

People can try to tell you what to do and how to feel both during and after a crisis, but no one knows how you really feel except yourself. People are ready to give you a lot of free advice, but it is very important that you do what is best for you.

In order to help validate yourself as a good person, you might want to consider doing the following:

1. Write down ten good character traits about yourself.

2. Write down ten things you want to achieve.

3. Re-affirm for yourself that you are a good person exactly the way you are.

4. Use any method of relaxation to help overcome insecurity.

Nervous and Scattered Person

Some people are so nervous they can't even keep a job very long.

They jump from one project to another without finishing anything because they are so scattered. This is an employer's nightmare. Once an employer realizes how this person works, he will try to get rid of him without laying him off so he does not have to pay unemployment.

This person is a nervous wreck. You can't say anything to him because he'll jump you. He has mood swings. The reason for this is often because of something organically wrong with him. But this is really up to his physician to say.

Nonetheless, this person does have to watch their diet. They should avoid drinking too much coffee or caffeine. They should cut down on the intake of sweets. They should not smoke cigarettes.

This person also needs to exercise. Walking is the best.

They also should drink a lot of water, for the electrolytes, in order to keep their system clean and in balance.

They have to make sure they get at least eight hours sleep. If they don't do this, they can't function very well at all. As a result, they will be tired all day long. No employer, and not even another employee, will want to have them around because they drag the entire rest of the staff down. They are not very productive anyway, but if they don't have sleep, they are even worse.

Friendship

You have to treat your friends nicely. Otherwise, your friendships won't last and you'll never get your friends back again.

If you don't want to be friends with someone anymore, just pull away. You don't have to be mean to them.

Don't use people because it will come back around to you. Don't make an enemy of a friend. That's one of the worst things you can do.

Friends are important. They have a different relationship with you than your family. A good friend can be invaluable to you for good advice. You'll appreciate them in a time of rejoicing or in a time of a crisis.

Remember, we are all trying to get through life and we each have our own difficult times. We have to try to help those who help us and to try not forget those who show us kindness.

Don't back stab those who helped you. No only is it not right or justifiable, but just because you don't need that friend right now, you might need them someday. If you back stab them, you will lose them forever. Treat others the way in which you wish to be treated.

Friendships can be valuable in helping you get through problems. It is also a true test of a friendship to see how a person reacts to your problems.

One should try not to lean too heavily on friends, but it is comforting to know that your friends are there for you. During a crisis, you should develop a support system with a close friend whereby you call them at regular times, either once or twice a day, just to "check in" and let them know how you are doing.

When you have money, all of your "friends" will call you all of the time. They'll want to be with you all of the time. You'll get invited to all of the parties. Your phone won't stop ringing. They'll want you to go shopping. They'll want you to have lunch.

Wait until you have nothing. It's a rude awakening. You realize that they are only there for the good times. If you tell them about your problem when you have one, they say they'll call you, but you'll never hear from them.

Sometimes even your own kids don't want to be bothered if you have a problem.

Sometimes your friends might have problems themselves, but they won't talk about them. If you don't talk about yours, they might think you have no problems either. You'll look good to them. You can laugh and have fun and you can invite them over to entertain them. You cook, prepare all the food, and provide the liquor and everything seems fine.

There was a married couple who was very wealthy and who did a lot of entertaining. They had a huge home. When they entertained, they spent a lot of money and made many special preparations.

Then they bottomed out financially. The husband wasn't working. The wife got sick from alcohol poisoning and she eventually died. At her funeral only five people showed up.

Sometimes the good hearted suffer too.

If you don't pay attention to those who help you when you are down, you will not succeed. What comes around, goes around. Don't think you are up there above others because as soon as you start thinking that way, you're one step closer to your own demise.

Remembering Yourself

Sometimes you are working so hard that you forget yourself.

If you have a little money set aside, take some time to enjoy yourself. Go get a manicure or a pedicure, go to a movie—even by yourself. Don't worry about the money. Remember to pamper yourself.

Sometimes you don't want to do anything anymore. You just procrastinate and throw things around and aren't really focused. You pile everything up. You are by yourself. You have no one.

You need something new to get yourself going and to get yourself inspired. The best thing you can do is to take care of yourself.

If you have overcrowded things in your life, it's a big job to straighten everything out again. It's overwhelming. It is much easier if you constantly stay organized on a daily basis than if you try to do it all at once.

Emergency Money

A single person has to save money.

Make sure you always have some cash around. What happens if one day you cannot work any more or if you get sick? Sometimes you can be afraid of what's going to happen to you, but don't be afraid. If you save some money, you won't have to worry.

While you are working, you need to save some money. You bring home a paycheck every week; you can put away savings. You don't know what the future holds. You think you have job security, but this is not always the case. If anything happens to your job, you need to have money for those rainy days.

Don't touch this money unless you have a health emergency or another "real" emergency, or if you need absolute necessities. This does not mean borrowing from this account for frivolous things such as clothing, shoes, or other non-essential items.

It's actually best to separate emergency funds from your regular savings. You can save this money in the bank and still get interest. Don't just leave the money there without accumulating interest. You can put it in a certificate of deposit account, which yields a higher interest, but you will have to resign yourself to leaving it there for an extended period, anywhere from three months to ten years or more. You decide the length of time that is most comfortable for you.

If you withdraw your money early, you incur a penalty that deducts money from the interest you can earn. The longer the time you put the money in the bank, the higher the yield. You can open two or more accounts with shorter and longer periods of investment. This is advisable if you think you'll have to withdraw some of the money because there won't then be a penalty on all of your interest, only on some of it.

The only way to know what you spend is to write it down. Otherwise, you have no idea. Keep a small notebook in your pocketbook to mark down your daily expenses and transfer it to your permanent record when you get home at night. You can put it in a ledger or log it in a file in your computer (but remember to keep a back up copy on a floppy disc).

When you are twenty to thirty, you should start saving for your retirement. Save as much as you can. That is very important. When you reach fifty to sixty, try very hard not to spend money.

A woman must save money. She must prepare. She should buy good jewelry that she can sell if she needs to. She can use it as an investment.

You can always make money in this country if you want to work. The United States is a beautiful country, although some people do not appreciate it.

Bankruptcy

In the past, bankruptcy has been a devastating experience for the parties going through it.

When you marry someone, you could be effected by an earlier bankruptcy. If one party has gone bankrupt and you buy a house together, then you pay more because the interest rate is higher due to the bankruptcy. It's better that you don't jointly buy the house. If you really want to go in with him, though, don't put his name on the papers until after the bank has approved the mortgage. Then you can still get the low tax rate.

How to Save Money

Shop wisely.

When you go to a store, look for sales.

Stick to your color and a style that is classic, not trendy. Try the clothes on before you buy them.

You can dress very well. Only buy the best, but limit the quantity. You only need four dresses: one black, one brown, one off-white, and one red.

Buy a few nice suits. Buy skirts and blouses with the idea in mind of mixing and matching them.

You don't need to buy very high heel shoes. Buy medium sized heels so you can wear them in the daytime, too. Stick to the colors you love.

CHAPTER VII
HEALTH

Take Care of Yourself

If you don't take care of yourself first, you can't be there for anyone else. This cannot be emphasized enough.

People have a tendency to wear you down if you let them. Learn how to say "no" if you do not have time or if something is not convenient or acceptable to you.

You learn how to be the master of your own fate. No one else is going to try to make you happy except yourself. You have to know and define what you want, and then go after it. You must know who you are. Don't forget where you came from. Your roots are part of you.

You have to know how to entertain yourself, too. It's important. That's one way of taking care of yourself.

Do not neglect your looks, your body, your face, or your diet. If you feel good about yourself, it does not matter what other people think. Don't let anyone tell you what to do. Be your own person and be true to thy self.

Don't let anything bother you. Don't get stressed. Don't worry. If you don't finish what you are working on today, tomorrow is another day.

Knowing how to relax is important in taking care of yourself. Find a quiet place where you can be alone. Put on comfortable clothing. Light two or three candles. Lie down for awhile on your back with your arms a few inches from your side on a softly carpeted floor.

Be strong inside and outside. You need to protect yourself from any damaging things, especially in today's world. It is not like the old days. With today's relationships and sexual relationships, people aren't as careful.

Some men do not involve their emotions when you have sex with them. They don't care what happens to you after. Everything becomes your problem. They don't take things seriously. They do things at the moment for random pleasure without regard for the consequences. Their philosophy is "tomorrow is another day." These men are still emotionally immature so it's easy for them to walk away if some little thing bothers them. For you this sexual excitement can then cause problems like disease, pregnancy, fear, and disappointment.

There was a man like this who said his fiancée was the most important thing in his life before he got married. Now that they've been married twenty years, he's turned into a selfish ogre.

She comes last: after his parents, after his friends, after his job, after his car, even after his bad golfing. He spends more time with the kids than with her. When she asks him where she comes in, he just complains about his work and boasts about what a good guy he is. She begins to wonder if men become more selfish as they become older?

People with Allergies and Stomach Problems

Diet can often have the most direct and immediate effect on your well being. A healthy body must start with a healthy diet.

"You are what you eat," is an old adage, but it is literally true because the cells in your body are constantly being replaced by the molecules in your food. Food supplies the building blocks in the chain of amino acids and essential fatty acids that repair and replenish your tissues.

Eliminating junk food from your diet leaves you with the most delicious food in the world.

Keep a healthy diet that is balanced between the five tastes that are the sweet, the salty, the bitter, the sour, and the hot. Do everything in moderation. You do not need to be a macrobiotic vegetarian, but meat and fish should be kept to a minimum and balanced by whole grains and vegetables.

Eat a lot of fruit and drink a lot of water to clean your system. Avoid ice cream and any food or drink that comes straight from the refrigerator. Your beverages should be room temperature because cold beverages impair the abilities of the spleen and the functions of the stomach. Cut down on dairy products, too, particularly if you suffer from cataracts, indigestion, or allergies.

Avoid citrus, catsup, vinegar, peanuts, peanut butter, cheese, wine, beer, sweets, bananas, milk, meat, eggs, white flour, caffeine, honey, molasses, maple syrup, and any junk food.

Milk should be avoided when you are ill.

Fresh fruit has sugar, but it also has fiber, so enjoy it, especially in the summer when it is grown locally and is ripe. But don't eat fresh fruit on an empty stomach.

Keep Yourself Looking Young at Any Age

It is very important to exercise and to keep your weight down. This is true for all women, but it seems to be more important for single women. Watch what you eat. Sometimes, if you gain weight in the wrong places, it is very hard to correct this. If you smoke, you get lines before your time. Sunbathing is very bad for you, too, unless you use a sun block of 40-50.

Don't mix alcohol with medications. Don't stay up late at night. You must go to sleep early. This is very important. If you require eight hours of sleep a night, then be certain to get that much sleep. Otherwise, you will be operating on overdrive. You can do this for a night or so, but not consecutively. You'll burn yourself out and the results will be obvious. It is hard to recapture this loss of sleep. Be sure not to party too much because this can take its toll on you, too, and age you.

When you become a certain age, you tend to walk differently. You have to learn how to walk with the correct posture. Have your shoulders back and your chest out. Swing your arms.

The clothes you wear are important, too. Don't wear too much black. If you do wear black, make sure you mix it with a color. If you are feeling down, never wear black.

If you think you have gained a little weight, then you should meditate with the idea in mind that you are thin again. This will help you lose weight.

Women must exercise. Walk every day or every other day. Join a club where they have group exercises and dancing. Have fun while you are exercising. Music is good for the soul. Dancing to music helps keep you young.

Moisturize your skin two to three times a day.

To keep your weight down, avoid sweets, fats, dairy, caffeine, alcohol, and carbohydrates. Stay away from junk food and fast food.

Take care of your hands and feet. Maintain good dental care.

Avoid emotional stress as much as possible. Make sure you don't worry too much. Worry is very bad for you, as it creates so much stress within you. If you know of or can anticipate a situation that is likely to be stressful, avoid it. You'll usually know in advance if you listen to your inner self.

Some of us have a powerful psychic energy which, if we tap into it, can help guide us to where we want to be at the time we want to be there. Sometimes we don't want to listen, and we are sorry for it later on.

Stress can make you so sick you cannot function. You cannot think straight. It takes a toll on you. If you get into a bad situation, either in a relationship or in a situation where you do not feel comfortable, do the best you can to extricate yourself from it. Otherwise, you won't be able to do your job efficiently, and every time you do something, you'll make a mistake.

When you are stressed, you can gain weight or lose weight.

Start using eye cream at the age of twenty to slow down the appearance of crow's feet. You should also limit your exposure to the sun. If you are taking any medication, avoid any exposure to the sun because you can get dark spots and these brown spots can lead to broken capillaries. If your eyes become dark, that means you have poor circulation. Try not to squint or make faces, otherwise you can get wrinkles in those areas. Make sure you use sunscreen and never burn your face or your skin because the effects are irreversible.

When you wake up in the morning and your eyes are puffy and baggy, that can mean your pillow is too low. You are retaining water. You can press your first two fingers into your leg to see if you are retaining water.

You need water, but mostly drink tea, fruit juice and other liquids, not just straight water. Never drink tap water.

If your skin is pale and wrinkled, that means you have poor circulation. Don't eat raw food. Eat only room temperature food.

When You Are Sick

You can learn to read your body.

For example, when you go to the bathroom, check your urine. If it is very yellow, then you could have an infection.

Look at your skin. If your skin is pale or yellow, then you need to take vitamins.

If you have circles around your eyes, then you may need to get extra sleep and stop worrying so much. You should also have your blood checked by the doctor. Don't wait long to do this after you first notice the circles.

If you taste salt when you taste your sweat, that means you are just perspiring because of the heat. If you don't taste like salt when you sweat, that means you are sick. Don't touch alcohol, sweets, milk, or raw food until you get better.

Body and Mind/Meditation and Self Healing

If you are not feeling well or if you are stressed, you cannot do certain things. Your mind isn't clear and alert. If you drink too much alcohol, smoke or worry, you cannot do things very well either.

At these times meditation is beneficial.

When you meditate, you must be relaxed. Turn your phone off. Light a candle. One purpose for meditation is to ask for something, but first you have to decide what you want. You can't ask for too many things.

In order to heal yourself from a traumatic break up or a bad experience, try to incorporate the following regimen into your daily activities: exercise, hot baths with aromatherapy and candles, meditation, and positive thinking. Choose creative pastimes for yourself, too, which involve something you love or at least enjoy doing. It could be something you have dreamed about doing or some wish you have been longing to fulfill.

After 5:00 p.m. light candles and incense and have a glass of your favorite beverage, either a special concoction or even wine. Make life fun even when you are home by yourself. Learn to enjoy your own company. Put on some relaxing music, something soothing that warms your soul and makes you feel happy and alive.

If you are home alone and are playing music, pretend you are a young woman again. It's good for your spirit. Dance to the music.

After you have been sitting down to have lunch or dinner, move around. Don't just sit in one place when you finish.

There is an ancient Chinese method of meditation that will give you an answer every time. People do it now more than ever and it can work for you. If you want to forget something bad that you have in your head, start concentrating. Sometimes you have it in your mind that you are feeling bad only because your have been feeling bad for so many years. Just make yourself try to forget that. Whatever you do, do not put anything else bad in your mind. Instead, put into your mind something that you did in your past at a happy time. Be patient. Sooner or later, it will diminish.

This will help transform you. You will be a different person. Whatever you feel, you can take yourself there mentally. Don't tell yourself that you can't do it. If you put it in your mind, you will get it because you ask for it.

Sometimes you'll feel that you can fly in the air. You won't grow wings, but you'll feel like you can fly.

When you begin to meditate, make sure you have solitude, peace and quiet. Otherwise, it will not work. Wait for the appropriate time in which to do it.

It is very important that you nurture your body, too, for meditation. If you have a heavy meal, have green tea afterward. This also kills fat. If you want to take vitamins, don't take too many. Some foods can hurt you. When you are not feeling good, don't touch dairy products. They can be a disaster to your system. Boil water when you don't feel well. If you want tea, make it very mild. Don't drink too much coffee. Take only a little, and only in the morning.

In the daytime, meditate silently. If you want to lose weight, picture yourself when you were very thin and happy. If you picture a person that you have not seen for a long time, eventually they will come to you. If you haven't seen a boyfriend for a long time, sooner or later he will come to you right before your eyes. You have to be very serious about this. Meditate and it will come to you. It does not just have to be a person. It could be something else.

Before you do this kind of meditation, you have to burn incense and play soft music.

In the nighttime, when you meditate, alternate night by night between using sound and not using sound in your breathing. When you inhale, you do so through your nose silently. When you exhale your breath, you make the sound of "ohm," called a mantra.

Meditation is very good for asthma. It will help you clear your lungs. Light unscented candles, but you only need to use these candles at nighttime.

Walk for an hour to an hour and a half every day. It gets your metabolism going.

Exercise is a necessity and all exercise is beneficial, but you also need to find a system that works with "subtle energy." Yoga is an excellent form of this kind of exercise.

Worry, grief, fear, and anger are all possible causes of disease. However, since fighting these disturbances itself creates even more conflict, it is more important just to quietly recognize, without any effort, and be aware of your problems. In this way, they will become quiet and naturally abate, just like a restless horse let loose in a large meadow that eventually becomes calm and begins to graze.

Meditation is a time-honored way of achieving this goal.

Protect Your Body

When the weather is extreme, it is important to protect yourself against the elements. If it is cold, you must bundle up. It is particularly important to keep your neck, your shoulders, and your lumbar region warm. Always wear a scarf on windy or cold days. Make sure that you don't have a gap between your top and your pants.

If you have problem areas such as sore knees or ankles, keep them especially warm.

Feng Shui

Feng Shui is a wonderful old Chinese philosophy. It is founded upon the principle of simplicity.

If you get into it, it can help you tremendously. The philosophy is centered on the precept that you shouldn't accumulate a lot of clutter in your life. If you have accumulated clutter, you should address the reason why you have done so.

Eliminating the clutter can be a very cleansing experience. "Now" is always a good time to clean out the clutter in your house, your basement, your attic, or anywhere else it has accumulated.

In Feng Shui anything metallic signifies the activation of wealth. In Asia people often put on their walls coins that are interconnected with a red thread.

An aquarium with fish strongly activates the wealth element, too. In your office aquarium place eight goldfish and one black fish. At home, two goldfish and one black fish. The water and goldfish represent money. The black represents your career. If the fish die, you have to replace them right away. Don't wait.

If you have a waiting room in your office, just put magazines in it. Don't crowd the table.

In the home, the master bedroom should ideally be located behind the central meridian of the house. It should also be located obliquely to the front door of the house so that one can control one's destiny. When possible, situate the master bedroom as far away from the front door and from the road as possible so there is peace and harmony within the house. The closer the location of the bedroom to the front door, the less peace people will feel there. If the bed is far away from the entrance, people will also feel more peace and security.

The bathroom and the kitchen should not be located along the central line of the house or the occupants can become ill along the center line of their bodies.

Music

Music effects positive changes in our psychological being and in our physical, cognitive, and social functions. Because music accesses so many different parts of the brain, its effect is profound on our emotional and physical lives.

Music directly stimulates our emotions and imagery. Music also has a direct effect on the body. Music is actually as efficient and quick as other established methods of relaxation such as meditation or yoga. Music can lower high blood stress levels and can induce muscle relaxation. In fact, music reduces stress so effectively that the levels of stress hormones actually sink.

It is more beneficial for you to listen to live music when you can. It's nice to go to a club where they have singers on stage and listen to them. This gives you a night out and it is relaxing as well as entertaining. Listening to people sing live is different than listening to the stereo. It relieves your stress more completely.

Being Independent

Men like it if you are independent.

They like it if you can take care of yourself and not be too needy. It makes their lives easier and less worrisome.

It's a wonderful thing to become independent. Then whatever you do, you won't make a lot of mistakes.

If you can find a man, that's great. If not, then that's okay too. Maybe some of us are meant to be alone.

When you have struggled in the past, it has not been right for you. Now that you know why these past relationships did not work out, you have the experience you need to succeed, either with a man or by yourself.

Learn to Find a Quiet Place Within Yourself

You have to learn how to be in control of yourself, whether you are in some hectic situation or just at work, on the highway, or socializing with friends.

Some quiet activities that may help you are prayer, meditation, chanting, deep breathing, relaxation exercises, visualization, candlelit bubble baths, exercise, short naps, or any other activity that makes you remember who you are. Take care of yourself on a daily basis. Nurture your soul.

You need to know that you can be happy by yourself.

Use the following meditation technique as part of a cleansing regime. Light candles beforehand, but don't use scented candles. Besides putting a candle in the room you are meditating in, put two candles in the kitchen, as well, and three candles in the living room from 5 p.m. to 7 p.m. Burn unscented or musk incense.

Then, to ease any strain on your legs, sit on a straight-backed chair with both feet flat on the floor. Cross your hands in front of you, close your eyes and direct your attention inward.

Feel the strong foundation of your buttocks, legs and feet as they make contact with the cushion and the chair. From this firm base, allow your spine to seem to float gently upward without strain on the legs. Let go of any force.

Now begin to focus on your breath.

Here is another exercise to help you find a quiet place within yourself. A yogi calls this position the corpse. Lie on the floor face up. Your feet should be about twelve inches apart and relaxed. Your eyes must remain closed at all times. Breathe deeply. Inhale and exhale. Concentrate on your breathing. Allow your body to find its own breathing rhythm and then feel and hear that rhythm. Imagine that as you inhale, your breath fills your lower abdomen. Inhale and exhale very slowly.

Then contract and relax every muscle of your body, one after the other, working from your toes to the top of your head.

Then begin to visualize your past, when there were happier times in your life. Visualize your friends or your loved ones.

Expectations

You need to come to accept certain things in life.

How much energy are you willing to devote to that which is beyond your reach and understanding? If you can stop expecting anything from anyone other than yourself, you can let go and move in a forward direction. You can channel your energy toward your own life.

Your allegiance to yourself must come first, before any allegiance to anyone else. You must make your allegiance to your own inner soul. This is critical. Don't forget it.

Following in Your Parents' Footsteps

Some children have parents who are doctors, lawyers, or wealthy entrepreneurs. These parents always give their children money, but they can ruin them by doing this.

The children begin to feel like big shots if the parents give them too much. They walk around and act like they are the ones who made the money, when it was in actuality their parents who did. This is referred to as "riding the coattails."

They don't pay too much attention in school, so they are not good students. They develop an attitude. They don't want to work. After all, why should they when they can get their parents to dole out the money to buy them anything they want? Unfortunately, this is the only life they know.

Their parents have to be strict with them and make them work. If they have worked for the money, then they have values and they will always watch their money.

If the parents have inherited the money or if they are nouveau riche, they don't really know the concept of money. They too have no responsibility whatsoever. They never know what's going to happen to them. Eventually their money runs out. They don't know what to do. They are not resourceful and they don't know how to pick themselves up.

When the parents have started a business, as long as it is successful, it is much easier for the children than starting their own business. Their street is already paved. Sometimes these children feel that if they follow in their parents' footsteps, they won't have to struggle and they'll have an easy time of it. However, to be successful they have to be just as diligent and conscientious as their parents were. They have to respect the foundation of the enterprise that their parents started.

CHAPTER VIII
RELATIONSHIPS WITH
CHILDREN

Professional Mothers and Their Interactions with Their Children

This can be a difficult mixture.

The mother is very busy and she is intellectually oriented toward business. The children can resent the mother's intelligence and the mother's business interests. They can become arrogant toward their mother and constantly bully her and hurt her feelings.

They'll do whatever the mother does not want them to do.

They do not do well in school because they want attention. They want the mother to feel sad for them. They have no concept of what it is to support themselves.

This mother works hard because she wants to give her children a good life with the best that she can provide, but sometimes her children do not really appreciate her. They take her for granted. The mother buys them the best clothes and shoes. She gives them spending money. She does whatever she can within her abilities.

These children then get used to having their mother take care of them and they do not want to go to work when they are of a working age.

The mother can then try to discipline them by reducing the expensive things she purchases for them and reducing the amount of spending money she gives them. When she does this, though, the children become furious with her. If there is a father in the picture, the children will go to him to get money for what they want.

This creates a conflict between the parents because they disagree with each other regarding their parenting skills. The children play one against the other.

If the parents really want to discipline these children, they have to sit down and discuss exactly how they want to raise them.

Single Mothers

If you are a single mother, your children won't always appreciate you.

Children need a lot of attention, every minute, every day, every year. As soon as you close your eyes to them, everything goes "boom." You have to listen to them, and you have to talk to them.

You love them and you want to discipline them so they can make it in life. However, sometimes the more you discipline them, the more they don't like you.

Children should not move out unless they have a good job. They have to be able to take care of themselves.

Sometimes a daughter will live with a man without being married. If she's not careful, she will have a baby when the two of them are not ready for it. Because they are so young, they think the baby is a toy, but the baby is not there just for one day. The baby is there for twenty-four hours each day, every day.

Their problems have arrived. You try to guide them, but they won't listen. They have to do everything their own way.

When they grow up, they finally say, "You were right." They start using all your words with their children when they are about forty or fifty. Sometimes then there is a happy ending for the mother and the kids both.

In the Orient, girls do not have sex until they get married. They have to be virgins when they get married. Parents are strict with their daughters and very careful when they are growing up. The daughters have no social life outside their parents' home when they become teenagers.

They don't let their daughters go out by themselves. Everywhere they go, the parents go with them, and even in the daytime the parents go out with them until they get married. In the Oriental culture, sometimes the parents are held accountable for the children's actions, too.

In America, if parents are religious, they are very serious with their daughters. They watch them closely, like hawks. If their daughter goes out with friends, they do not allow her to stay out too late. The bottom line is usually 12:00 p.m., unless she is with friends she has known for a long time or if she is in a committed relationship.

In America many girls have had several sexual partners by the age of twenty. Most women are either married by then or have children or live with men without the benefit of marriage even though they have children.

They have not even started their career. They don't take their time to really work on themselves.

Men don't have to worry about children and marriage as much as women. They don't have to have responsibility for a woman if they don't marry her. They can walk out more easily and the woman may not see them again. Women have to worry about what is going to happen to them and the children.

Sometimes girls think of babies as dolls. They don't realize that a baby changes them for the rest of their lives, not just for a day or for an hour, but forever. A mother's job is a non-stop, twenty-four hour a day task.

Daughters only know who their mothers are after they have gone through motherhood, and the only way they really know what their single mothers have gone through is when they have to start paying the bills themselves. Then they realize what a hard time their mothers had raising them by themselves.

Single Parents with Children in College

When your children go to college, do they know what they are doing?

You want your children to find a job when they get out of school, but the children have to figure what out they want to do before they go to college. They need to develop a curriculum and stay with it. They have to be focused.

If you aren't careful, you can be fostering your child's role in school as a "professional student." They become able to "ride the wave" and not be focused on doing anything except having the parents pay their bills. Parents must really instill in the children how important it is to take their education seriously.

Their children need to decide on a career and stick with it. Unfortunately, the only time they are really going to start to understand is when they start to pay their own bills. Then things will really start to hit home for them.

Children don't always appreciate what their parents do on their behalf. Children have to learn how to value their parents, not abuse them. They need to treat them with respect because they do so much for them and give up so much in order for them to have it better than the parents did.

If parents give their children advice, the children must learn how to listen to them. That advice is not just from books, and the parents give it because they want their children to do better and because they love them.

Unfortunately, children sometimes resent the advice given by the parents. They are rebellious. They think they know better. They are reluctant to heed their parents' experience.

Their values are different because they are influenced by their peers and by the strong messages that are being sent through advertising and through television in general. They receive the message that they will receive happiness and instant gratification by obtaining some thing, some possession or material wealth. They get caught up in the vicious cycle of wanting to obtain more and more "things." The concept they are given is that more is better.

This message is sent because large corporations control our society; however, most of them don't care about the values and social mores in our society. They care about making themselves more profitable.

Isn't it natural, therefore, for children to equate happiness with "things"? Besides that, as children, they know they are not themselves paying for the "things," so what difference does it make? At that age their objective is centered not on earning the money to go buy the "things" themselves, but on how to become masters at convincing their parents they as children <u>need</u> these items in order to survive.

They don't even stop to analyze the difference between what they need and what they want.

Some children don't need to go to college. Some children are not good in school. No matter how much you force them to go, it just will not work. It's a waste of your breath.

Those kids may not be academically inclined, but they are inclined to take classes at trade or technical school. They prefer to learn a trade rather than to go to an ivory tower school.

Daddy's Princess

Because she does not want to lose her father, a "daddy's princess" thinks that her divorced daddy should never meet any other woman.

This child is very controlling, yet the father is ready to spoil her every need and want. He can be so willing to keep her around that he will put an apartment is his house for her. He should never do that. She'll think she can live with him for the rest of his life.

There was a woman who did nothing but stare out the window because she was so lonely. She finally took a job, but she lost it because she became very sick.

She started getting lonely again. Then she became sick. She had no one to come and be with her. Nobody was there for her and she became even more lonely.

Her children tried to provide company for her because she was so lonely.

She was afraid she would never meet anyone because her children were now always catering to her, but finally she met a gentleman. They dated for a while and then she took him to meet all her family.

He would not let her meet his family, though, because of his daughter.

One day he said to this woman, "I want to spend my life with you. We are going to be very comfortable and happy."

He sat his daughter down and told her that things had changed. He wanted to spend his life with this wonderful, beautiful woman that he had met. The daughter said she did not want her father to marry the woman. He had to take a strong stance with her so that she would not interfere with his life. He told her that he was going to marry her because he did not want to lose this woman.

In reality, this fostered his daughter's independence. It also allowed the father to have the relationship he deserved with a new wife.

If his relationship with his new wife was not only going to survive, but thrive, he and his daughter had to have autonomous lives. He could still see his daughter as much as was comfortable, but she couldn't interfere with his marriage. She couldn't be allowed to undermine his love for his new wife or ultimately their marriage would fail.

When Your Kids Forget You

It is not right when children forget their parents. They should respect their parents and help them. They should remember all the sacrifices the parents made in order to give them a better life.

Teenagers Who Leave Home

Children become emancipated, generally and legally, at 17. They are free then, so there is nothing you can do to stop them if they want to leave.

If the children have a problem, though, it can become your problem. The society and even your friends and family may be apt to blame you, even when it's not your fault. Just prepare yourself for the worst. This is a very rough period in a teenager's life, both for the teenager and for the parent.

You have to watch teenagers all the time, but especially before puberty. When they are eight, nine or ten, a mother needs to stay close to them, especially to her daughters.

When they reach thirteen and fourteen, they start getting wild and crazy ideas, so you have to watch their friends, too.

Teenagers cannot wait to reach seventeen or eighteen and to be "adults." They want freedom because they think their parents are very strict. They don't like to be told what to do, so they can't wait to get out of the home.

Sometimes they move out without their mothers' and fathers' permission. They don't care if they only have a dollar in their pocket. They don't have a job or a profession.

Sometimes they tell their friends about you and about the terrible things you did. They like you to get in trouble.

You have tried so hard to protect them because you want what's best for them so they can have a better life. But teenagers can be very rebellious, especially teenage girls.

If you are a single mother, it is generally worse with a teenage girl at home. She can give her mother a very hard time.

When teenager girls leave home, they are not usually prepared. They might wind up living with a guy. Sometimes they don't get married and yet they have children. Then problems start. Some girls have a baby and then they go out and get a job.

It is hard for the children and hard for her, but if she stays home and takes care of the children, she does not get paid. She goes out to find a job, but she has no experience, so she takes whatever job she can get. She does things she is not supposed to do. It's hard for her even to afford a babysitter.

The teenage girl's children struggle, too, when they only have a single parent because money is usually tight. In these cases the girl should make the guy marry her so she can have a future.

Children should not have to struggle like that. As teenagers they might believe their parents are bad, but when they go out in the real world, they find out what life is all about. They realize that their parents only meant the best for them and that their parents love them. That's the reason why they tried to discipline them.

The love you get from your parents is different from the love you get outside. After you go out there and you need help, the first one to help you is your mother. She will be there before your friends are.

Children should listen to their parents because they have been around a lot longer. It's true that children don't know any better because they are young, but children today should really listen to their parents.

They should not leave home until they at least have five months rent in the bank and they should have a job at the same time. They could even have two jobs. If they only work part time, they should go to school and develop a career or a trade to improve themselves.

You have to teach your children to be independent. That way they can be self-reliant. The best thing is to train yourself to be independent and self-sufficient. Then you can teach them.

Teenagers think they are going to be young all the time. They laugh and have a good time and time goes by very fast. Most teenagers don't take life very seriously. They are concerned with going places with their friends and having a good time. They typically go out and stay out late and sleep all day.

They usually stay within one crowd, but it can be confusing within that crowd. Sometimes they don't really see what is going on, and they can be led in the wrong direction by their peers

When teenagers finally start to take things seriously, they may realize they have lost time and now have to work hard to catch up.

Parental Love

Love from a parent is for ever and ever.

You can't get love outside your family the way that you do from your parents. Love from a parent goes deep within your head and within your heart.

Only after their children have grown up is it time again for the parents to do for themselves.

Single Parent Having Children when She is Young

A young girl needs to see the world; but if she gets pregnant, her life is never the same.

Her life can be done. Finished. She can be stuck for the rest of her life. It's hard for her to keep a decent job because she doesn't have enough schooling. People are apt to fire her for doing the least thing wrong. She works hard, but much of her money goes to the babysitter.

She is always worried about where she is going to get the money to pay the bills. She can become stressed and depressed. She has no life for herself, but there is no turning back.

It can be a thankless job. It could be wonderful, if she had the money, or if she had a partner to help her through the rough times. It's sad if she doesn't. If she gets sick, who is going to help her?

It can be very, very difficult.

When you are young, you can have a fantasy of the ideal world in which to have a child; but it is much different than that if you have no money.

Single Parents with Teenagers

Parents who are too busy tend not to pay attention to their teenagers; but teenagers have to be watched.

They can trick you into thinking everything is okay when it is not. They like to be like adults, even though they don't really understand the consequences to them when they do something wrong. When they get into trouble, it is trouble for the parents, as well.

It is not a good idea for you to give your teenager a credit card. Only give them the money you can afford to give them for spending money. Give them a set amount each week.

When your teenage daughter tells you she is going to her girlfriend's house, you better check up on her to be sure she are really there. Chances are that she could be somewhere else getting into trouble.

You have to pay attention.

Men Who Get Women Pregnant out of Wedlock

Men can just walk away from the women they get pregnant. They can lose themselves out there in the world without ever paying any of the bills.

So be careful.

When You are Pregnant

When you're pregnant, your baby eats the same food you do.

You can't touch any liquor or any drugs when you are pregnant. Some mothers do drink wine and liquor when they are pregnant, so when the baby grows up, they like the taste of liquor and they can become alcoholic. Sometimes a mother is too busy when the children are growing up to properly watch and care for her children.

When you're pregnant, you cannot eat certain things if you want to keep the baby happy and alert. You can prevent future problems, too. Eat things in moderation. Eat a lot of vegetables and fruit, especially cantaloupe, watermelon and broccoli. They are good for you and for the baby. Avoid spicy foods, meat, alcohol, coffee, too many sweets, smoking, caffeine, and drugs. If you take a prescription, do so only if your gynecologist prescribes the medication.

When you are pregnant, you cannot be too emotional. You might want to cry, you might feel angry, you might feel depressed, but you have to try to be happy because whatever you do, the baby will be affected by your mood. If nothing else, listen to music.

It is very important to walk a lot so that you don't have to have a Caesarian. Walk every day, twice a day for 15-20 minutes. Clear your head as you walk.

Swim if you can. It is very relaxing and good for the baby and for you. You can meditate while you swim by listening to the rippling effects of the water.

You need to establish a routine for your life.

If you are having relationship problems, you have to block them out and think of yourself and the baby first so that you can get through it.

Single Mother

Sometimes children can really break their parents' hearts, especially a single mother who has no help. Some children will take advantage of that situation and make her life miserable. They take everything that they can from her. They don't care.

They want to have a good time with their friends and the mother works hard to support their activities, but she gets nothing in return.

When they grow up, they think more of her, but it does not matter. She is alone. She still works long hours to pay the bills and no one gives her a hand.

She has to be very strong.

Fathers Who Worship Daughters

Men can be very close to their daughters.

A man will even divorce his wife because he wants to stay close to his daughter. These men have fantasies.

There was a man whose daughter had terrible acne. She had told him, "If I don't clear up my face, I'll kill myself." He took his daughter all over the world for help. She finally found my clinic and I cleared up her skin. Diet was very important, but because she was stressed, her skin had become even worse. Stress does funny things. She visited the clinic every week at first and then every other week for three months.

When her acne was gone, she thought her problems were solved, but that was not the only thing that bothered her. There was much more to it than that. Her skin had been only one aspect of her problems.

Her father thought that he could keep buying her things to make her happy. Meantime, she kept driving her father crazy by having a lot of men. She went through men very easily. She was only eighteen and probably had gone through ten men already.

However, every time her father tried to date, she cried out, "Me, me, me." He was very cheap with the girlfriends, but not with her. He would think nothing of buying her another mink coat.

He had been a millionaire. The daughter never had to work. He bought her a big house. All she did was entertain her friends and have parties. That was all she knew.

Finally there was no more money. The daughter had spent it all. She had no concept of the value of money.

Her father died with no money. At the end he could hardly pay for his prescriptions. His ex-wife had had to help him pay for his medication when he got sick.

After the father had lost all of his money, his daughter and his ex-wife, her mother, got back together because the father was poor. She and her mother got along well. Originally the wife had had custody of the daughter, but the husband would never allow the wife to take her.

The daughter had used her father, and now she was using her mother. Her mother was giving her the money she had invested after her divorce, and her daughter was draining her nonstop.

This daughter will have a difficult time for herself or in her marriage. She is not going to find a man who will treat her the way her father did. She will always be disappointed.

She does not understand life.

Raising Your Baby

A single parent works hard for her children. She—or he—doesn't take vacations. All of her money goes to her children.

Sometimes she is too busy, though, to properly watch and care for her children when they are growing up, but kids love to do things they are not supposed to do. You have to watch them like a hawk.

Children with Alcoholic Parents

If both parents are alcoholics, the children grow up fast.

These parents neglect the kids because they are so busy having parties with their friends. Sometimes they have parties just so they can blend in with everyone else who is drinking. They are only trying to cover up, but it is not funny anymore. It is a sickness.

Their problems effect everyone around them, family and friends.

Sometimes an alcoholic husband fights in front of the kids. For the child that's called "the wrong place at the wrong time."

If a father is like that, just leave him. Let somebody else take care of him. The kids should not have to suffer because of an alcoholic. Just because one person has problems, why should the children have problems? Let him leave. Or her, if it's an alcoholic mother.

They have a disease that you can't kill. They drug themselves with Percocet and alcohol. They don't eat. They can't concentrate on anything, not even on their jobs. They don't go home from the party or the bar. They forget that they have a family. The kids are left to run wild.

The kids can't tell anyone because they are ashamed. They keep it hidden within them. If they're sick, they can't go to doctors. Sometimes they have to wear rags.

If an alcoholic father has a daughter at home, he sometimes no longer knows if she is his daughter or his wife. However, the girl will not tell anyone that her father has abused her because he will go to jail if she tells. The girl can grow up and become a lesbian because she doesn't like the opposite sex or she can end up just living by herself because of her father. She has scars that don't heal.

However, if the children get help early, you can fix this. You have a family and you have a responsibility in this world to help them

Famous Parents

Some parents are in the public eye because they are celebrities. Their profession is very hectic, and all their time is devoted to pleasing the public. They are very busy.

They can get so caught up in this lifestyle, though, and not just because of the money, that they don't even know who they are. They don't realize that their children are only going to be young once, and that their children need them. They are at home waiting for them and wanting attention from their parents.

They hardly see their children. The parents don't do it completely on purpose, but they have chosen the lifestyle. There are only certain talented people who can do what they do, and sometimes they can only do it for a certain length of time so they feel that they have to do it while they can. Life is tricky and it is not easy to be a parent with this kind of situation.

Sometimes children don't understand. When their children grow up, they will sometimes talk about how bad their parents were. Sometimes they will do crazy things as a reaction and to get attention, and this can mean big trouble.

Although these parents can work very hard so that their children don't have to struggle for money, their children need more than that. They don't need things.

They don't need love from strangers. They know if there is real love from their parents or not.

The children end up with everything they need except their parents' time. They grow up and they think that their parents didn't love them because they were neglected. The parents think that all the things they have provided for their children give them love.

The children grow up and go to college, but they don't go home because there is nobody there. They don't see their parents often because they think their parents don't love them. After college, they get a job and move far away. Sometimes they don't even send their parents a post card.

The children have grown up, but don't have a true sense of what love is. Nor do they appreciate what their parents did do for them.

These parents want their children to have everything that they didn't have when they were little so they give them money and credit cards. They don't understand that showering their children with material things is not love.

Their children end up not understanding what life is all about until they get a job and support themselves. They have been taken care of all of their lives. They don't realize until they pay all of the bills and raise their own children what their parents did for them.

If they don't make it out in the world, they think their parents will support them. It takes them a long time to succeed in life sometimes.

Good parents love their children. They naturally worry about them and about what will happen to them in life. It is tough out there. Their children sometimes don't realize that no matter what happens in life, their parents will always love them. If they need help, their parents will always be there for them.

The best thing you can do is to make friends with your parents, because although you can choose your friends, but you cannot choose your parents.

There were two kids who grew up in a good family. Their parents educated them. They went to college. After they graduated from college, their parents still supported them until they had a solid foundation in life. They moved away from home, but they visited their parents a lot.

Much later, the children finally understood what their parents had gone through.

When their parents got older, they lived close to them. They took care of them. They took them on vacations. They appreciated their parents so much more now that they had their own children.

Their parents enjoyed their grandchildren, too, and the grandchildren loved their grandparents. The grandparents took them everywhere they went, and the parents didn't mind because they were busy working. The grandmother got up early in the morning and took the children to school because she enjoyed doing it. She drove her grandchildren everywhere until they grew up.

One day the children went off to college and she didn't have them anymore. She missed them so much, she felt like she no longer had her job.

Every time the children came home from college on vacation, they went to see their grandmother. They adored her. Even after the children got married, they took their grandmother to their homes a lot.

They are all a very happy family.

Her Mother is Very Important to Her

There was a woman whose father died a long time ago. After he died, she took over the care of her mother. She visits her mother two or three times a week. She takes her out to dinner. She makes time to go see her mother and take her shopping. She is with her mother a lot because her mother is alone.

They get along very nicely together, too. They call each other a lot. They are good friends and can count on each other.

When her children were little, her mother was always there for them. Now she is happy to be able to take care of her mother in return. She likes to have her mother depend on her, but her mother helps her do a lot of things, as well.

Her husband is good with her mother, too. Her marriage is successful because she does things for her family and for her mother.

She has a big heart and she helps her friends, too. She's loyal to all the people she loves.

She has a happy family, but there are few families that are like this.

Gay Friends Who are Loyal to Their Friends

There was a woman who had two gay men as neighbors.

All of her children were grown and lived out of state. They worked and had their own families. They couldn't take much time from work to visit.

Her husband wasn't feeling well and she took care of him by herself.

Sometimes her neighbors knocked on her door and if she couldn't go out, they would go to get groceries for her. Her neighbors sometimes cooked the food for them, too, and when her husband was most sick, these two gay men cooked for them a lot of the time. She told them that they cooked better than she did.

These neighbors did more for them than her own sons had done. They were very good to them. They would go visit the couple on weekends and spend a lot of time with them. They all enjoyed each other's company..

She and her husband had been married for over 30 years when he died. Her neighbors were very supportive of her then, too. Sometimes she would cry just because these two people were so nice to her.

One time they called her and told her that they were going to take a trip. They told her not to ask where they were going, but that they had made the reservations. They paid for everything, and they told her to take only so much money. They went gambling, went to dinner, and then went walking on the beach.

Almost every time they went somewhere, they would take her with them.

She said that she was very fortunate to have this couple as friends and that they were the best friends she ever had.

After her husband died, they always kept her busy. If they were going to a movie, they would ask her if she wanted to come with them. They joked around a lot so she would forget what she had on her mind. They made her laugh. She said that she didn't know where they got their jokes, but they really made you laugh.

She said they were very warm people and very sensitive. She hoped she never moved from her house because these neighbors were so wonderful. If they every moved away, she said that she would move with them.

They were kind people. She said that these unusual friends would last forever. Without them, she said, that she would be very lonely, very sad and depressed.

Male Friend

There was a woman who had been living together with her boyfriend for five years. One day he suddenly informed her that he was leaving her and moving out of their apartment. She was not prepared. It all happened so fast.

She knew she could not afford to keep the apartment by herself. She didn't know what to do. She didn't have a job at that time because she had just gotten fired. Because he had become the center of her universe, she had very few friends. She had to give up her apartment and she had no place to live. She didn't have a lot of money. She was down.

This man broke up with her was because of his parents. They were against the relationship.

The couple had been talking about settling down and getting serious. She had planned to marry him. At that time, he had just graduated with an accounting degree, but he didn't make much money yet.

When he told his mother that he was going to marry this girl, his mother told him that she was going to disinherit him. She looked at this girl, who looked very pretty, and she knew automatically that she was going to be high maintenance. His parents were old fashioned and not liberal minded.

After her boyfriend moved out, the best thing that could happened to her did. Her good, loyal friend took her in. He was gay and he was the definition of "true friend" in the real sense of the word.

He had been friends with her for a long time. When either would have problems, they would talk to each other and give each other advice.

Her friend took her into his home and let her stay there until she could get on her feet, financially and emotionally. He took care of her. At that time she did not even have a car to drive. Wherever she needed to go, he would take her there.

Her friend told her to stop going out with men for a while. He told her to get a job, even a few jobs. He was like a brother to her. He told her that the next time she dated, he wanted to meet the man first and give her his seal of approval.

Gay men are sincere with their friends, have good hearts, and are very warm. They know how to talk to you.

This man treated her like his sister. If it weren't for him, she would have been in the street. He protected her. He talked to her like a sister. He told her that she couldn't stay home to cry and feel sorry for herself. She had one week to stay in bed, he said, and after that she had to go to work. He told her that she had to keep herself healthy and strong. He said that this experience would serve as a lesson for her, and that she would be even stronger because of it. He believed that the next time she went with a man, she shouldn't take him seriously unless he gave her a ring.

He told her to go and exercise and he even paid for her gym membership.

She went to exercise. She began working. She started feeling better. Her phone started ringing.

Five months went by and her ex-boyfriend had been trying to call her. When he finally got through, he asked her if her house was Grand Central Station, and told her that she shouldn't give her phone number out to so many people.

He apologized. He was sorry about the whole thing and that it shouldn't have happened the way it did. He told her that without her, things were not the same. He didn't realize that his life was going to change so drastically.

He asked her out to lunch so they could talk. She told him that she didn't want to go out to lunch with him.

He continued calling her and told her that everywhere he went was a party or a place that he used to take her. Everyone asked him how she was doing and where she was. He didn't realize that everyone loved her so much.

He started calling her four or five times a day. He really wanted her back.

He told her that if they got back together, he would buy them a big home in the country. He had started making a lot of money, but he didn't know that his money could not cure everything. He told her that now he could do the things that he couldn't do before because he had been financially dependent on his parents then.

She finally told him that he better stop calling her because he had already put her through so much pain. She had done so much to try to make him happy.

She told him that she had been dating another man for two months now and she thought that he was serious. She was happy. She had a solid man who had a good job, and she wanted to marry him and have several children.

She told him that maybe it was not meant to be with him, but that she wished him well.

He was so sad that he went out drinking that night to help him forget what he now had on his mind. He hadn't realized that she was hurting so badly. He thought he was the only one who had gotten hurt and he hadn't known that she was hurting more than he was.

A year went by and this girl married her new boyfriend. She was happy and had nothing to worry about.

Two years more went by and her gay friend came to her and told her that his landlord was selling his apartment building because he was moving out of state. He told her that he needed a room.

She and her husband had a basement that was refinished. They made a deal with him that he would not have to pay anything for the studio, but that he would help the husband with the yard work. He not only helped out a lot in the yard, but he cooked beautifully for them too.

While he lived there, he saved all his money and in fifteen months he was able to buy a small house. He told her that he was tired of shuffling around in apartments.

Single Parents

There was a mother who was from Europe and she was very strict.

She realized her little girl was exceptionally smart as soon as she entered kindergarten. Her mother started to watch her like a hawk. She could not do the things other girls did. Her mother was too protective of her.

The little girl was very unhappy with her mother, and she grew to resent her because other children could do things that she wanted to do. She would always do things wrong just to spite her mother, to make her unhappy.

Her mother always watched the girl's diet. She only got food that was good for her, so her little girl would sneak other food. Her mother would give her an allowance every day and the little girl would buy food that she was not allowed to have. She was eight years old.

When her mother found out, she wouldn't give her money anymore.

One day she brought home some candy to sell door to door. Her mother bought all of the candy because she didn't want her to have to sell candy door to door. The little girl was so unhappy because she didn't get to sell any candy.

At eleven years old, the girl started smoking. She knew that she wasn't supposed to smoke and that it wasn't good for her. Her mother found the cigarettes in her purse and told her that her throat was not developed enough to smoke. She always sneaked cigarettes in her pocketbook after that. She wanted very badly to grow up.

By the time she was thirteen, her mind was way ahead of her age. She was so busy upsetting her mother that she never did her homework. Her teachers called her mother because she wasn't doing her work in school, but her mother was very busy working and couldn't really concentrate on her.

Her mother couldn't wait for the girl to grow up so she could help her with the house, the shopping and so forth. On the other hand, the girl couldn't wait to grow up and be an adult.

When she was older, the girl started working at a delicatessen so the mother stopped giving her an allowance. The girl got pudgy.

One day she asked her mother if she could go away with the other children on a trip. Her mother told her that she couldn't go with them. They argued and the girl called her father and told him to come and pick her up at the house. The father picked her up.

After a few hours the girl realized that she really didn't want to be with her father. She wanted to be home with the mother. She was only punishing her mother by doing what she did. Her father brought her home the same night. He didn't really want the responsibility of his daughter.

Her mother told her that the reason she hadn't wanted her to go away was because she felt that there wouldn't be enough adult supervision. However, she could have her girlfriend come over to the house.

While her mother cooked dinner, she and her girlfriend were talking about how their parents were. She told her girlfriend that she could not wait until she reached seventeen so she could leave home. The mother overheard the entire conversation. After that, her mother told her that she could not leave home at the age of seventeen because it was so dangerous out there. She said that she would run into problems outside.

The mother did not make a lot of money, but she managed to make enough money to take care of the girl. She worked hard for her and saved enough money to put her through college.

Her daughter didn't like school. In fact, she hated it, and when she turned seventeen, she finally ran away from home. She was emancipated. Her mother could no longer stop her from doing what she wanted to do. She had gotten her freedom.

She thought she would have a good life outside her home, and she went to live with her friend.

She wasn't very happy, though, because she didn't like to work. She didn't have any profession or training. She could not make enough money to support herself.

Her mother had always warned her about what could happen if she moved out because she couldn't get a job that paid well. She didn't respect her mother because she thought all her mother knew how to do was to cook and clean house. The girl had been so wound up to get her freedom that she had not been thinking straight.

Her mother was very upset. Her mother had worked so hard and sometimes had more than one job. She used to tell her daughter that when she grew up, they could work together and make their lives better.

Her daughter was still young. She didn't realize that her mother had overprotected her for her own sake. She thought she was now grown up and that she didn't need her mother. She still wouldn't follow her mother's directions.

After she moved out, her mother didn't talk to her for a very long time.

She got married and one day called her mother to tell her that she was pregnant. Her mother said simply, "Congratulations." She wouldn't go to see her because she was still very angry with her.

When the baby was about three months old, the daughter just stopped by to see her mother without calling her. Her mother didn't say anything, but she was so happy to see the baby that she forgot about everything in the past. Her mother actually had a weak spot for children and babies.

The daughter told her mother that she was now single and that she took care of the baby by herself. She said she hadn't known anything about motherhood until she had the baby.

She had always told her friends that she and her mother hadn't gotten along when she was growing up. Now she finally realized what her mother told her about how hard life was outside. It had become very hard for her, too. She hadn't realized it until she had a baby and had to take care of her by herself.

She now felt sorry about her mother. She realized how difficult she had been with her mother, who had to raise her as a single parent. Her mother had been very independent and hadn't relied on anyone any more than she had to. Mentally and physically, her mother was a very strong woman.

No matter how hard a time your children give you, you still try to discipline them. They may or may not listen, but at least you warn them about what could happen later on in life.

They won't forget you. Even when you are not around, they will always remember you and what you told them.

A Greenwich Family

There was a girl who grew up in Greenwich whose name was Donna. She was one of six children. Donna's mother was a good organizer and smart in business.

They had a big home in the back country with about five acres of land, an Olympic size swimming pool, tennis courts and a guesthouse.

Her maternal grandparents had been very wealthy. They owned a lot of the land in the Greenwich back country and, in fact, had practically owned half of the town at one time. They were very popular people.

Even though the grandparents were rich, they had taught the children to work and the children had all had a good college education. Donna's father listened carefully to his parents, and by following in their father's footsteps at their company, all the children made a lot of money.

Donna's father became a very successful man.

When the grandparents died, they left property to all of their children. Donna's father told her that none of the children would have to work for the rest of their lives because they now had enough money to support themselves.

Donna's mother and father were also very wealthy, of course, and Donna's mother didn't have to work, but she did anyway. She opened a company of her own and had many people were working for her. The company was based in New York, but they had divisions all over the world.

Because he had overworked himself, Donna's father died from a heart attack when she was nineteen or twenty years old. Her mother remarried, and her second husband was a little bit younger than she was. She already had four children, and then she had another child with her second husband, who was a lawyer. He worked in her company as their in-house counsel.

As the children grew up, the housekeeper helped raised them and they thought of her in many ways as their mother.

Donna's mother had an office in the home, but even though she was around a lot, she was not available to Donna or the rest of the children. She was busy with business meetings and with entertaining. She arranged beautiful parties, and the house always looked meticulous and the grounds looked beautiful, too.

Unfortunately, she did not discipline her children. All she did was tell the housekeeper to feed them, clothe them and take them to school. She never told her children that someday they must work.

On Sundays a minister would come out and they would have church services in their home.

When the children came to her for money, they never had to tell her what they were spending it on. All they had to do was ask for it. None of them had a job, even though they all went to college. They figured why should they work when they could get it for free. She never took her children shopping. She just gave them credit cards.

She had a driver at home, and a nanny, a housekeeper, a cook and a landscaper. She was friendly with Nancy Reagan. When Ronald Reagan was running for president, Donna's mother donated money to the Presidential Campaign Fund.

She gave a party two or three times a week. The children were around when liquor was being served and sooner or later, they started drinking right along with the guests.

Donna's mother started drinking with the guests, too, and eventually she became addicted to alcohol. She drank hard liquor, mostly vodka.

After she married her second husband, he started traveling a lot overseas and was hardly home at all. She didn't go away with him because she was so busy with the business and with orchestrating all the social activities at home. She acted like she was not lonely, but even though she had a lot of company, she was very lonely

Donna's mother began drinking more to combat her loneliness. She did not have any emotional support. Her new husband still had an apartment in Manhattan that he had had before he got married, and he stayed there in between his flights overseas.

Sooner or later, Donna's mother got into drugs, too. Once, when her husband did come home, he knew that there was something very wrong with her because she was very jumpy. She didn't act the same and her conversation was very different than before. He went into her dresser and found her Percocet. He knew that she had a problem and suggested that they get help for her.

However, her husband couldn't stay around because he was the only one who could actually handle the business. He had to go away for about a month, but when he came back, they went on vacation together.

When they got to their hotel, he noticed that she had brought a bottle in her suitcase. They had dinner invitations that night with people that they did business with, but she had gotten so drugged and drunk that he couldn't get her out of bed. He had to stay in the hotel with her because he didn't think it was safe to leave her alone.

He told her, "This trip may be about having a vacation, but it is also about business."

From there they went to Cuba, but they had to come home early because she was sick. When they got home, he tried to find help for her.

She would quit for four or five days and then go back to drinking again. Every time her husband opened the closets and looked in the dressers, he found more bottles and pills.

By this time all the girls had moved away from home and had gotten married. The boys still remained at home.

Every weekend the mother used to have parties with many guests. Her husband could no longer control her and couldn't do anything for her. She could not be helped because she liked the way she was. She had been drinking for a very long time, but everybody drank at the parties, so no one knew that she was addicted to it. She just gave up trying to quit. She went down hill and took more and more drugs and alcohol.

She died from the abuse.

She left each of her children a trust fund of one million dollars. They had been waiting for the money. Her children did not work at all even though some were thirty to forty years old. The boys still lived at home.

Her second husband retired. Over the years, he had developed an alcohol dependency, too. He had had an accident and sometimes his back bothered him terribly. Instead of going to the doctor, he drank to ease the pain. That was his medicine. He drank without eating and if he did eat, he didn't eat decent food, he just picked. The cook now only came to make meals three days a week, including the weekend.

One day he couldn't get out of bed. He called his daughter and told her that he needed a haircut. His daughter brought a girl named Theresa home to cut his hair. She was a foreigner. She cut his hair and manicured his nails.

From then on every time his hair got long, he would call Theresa to come to the house to cut his hair. Theresa was company for him. He enjoyed talking to her. She was good with people and he liked her.

Theresa had a full time job, but she took care of this client because he couldn't get out. Sometimes Theresa would go out and run errands for him when the help had the day off. He always asked Theresa if she wanted something to drink, but she declined. After she got to know him better, she would sometimes cook his dinner.

One night the man told Theresa, "When my wife died, everything stopped. The overseas business went downhill. The entertaining stopped. Our whole life changed. Our friends stopped coming over. Sooner or later, we sold the company for a billion dollars. It's very sad when a person has been so smart and has done everything. Not one of her five children followed in her footsteps. When she died, she died a lonely death. It looked like she had no one."

The problem was that the second husband was never around. The only thing he did then was to call home occasionally. She only had her pills and her bottle. She even slept with the bottle.

In the past, she had had many friends, but when she got sick, not many people sent her flowers or even a card. They had forgotten she was around.

The second husband and Theresa became friendly, but Donna had gotten jealous. All of his children were jealous of anyone he became friendly with because they didn't want anyone to go near him. They were afraid of losing the father's money, so Donna had a talk with Theresa and told her that she better stop seeing her father.

Theresa didn't tell Donna's father what the daughter said to her. She was afraid of what the children would do. He kept calling Theresa to ask her to come and cut his hair and to run errands.

Finally she went in spite of what Donna had said.

The children didn't really know Theresa, but she was not money hungry. She worked hard for a living and only got paid what she earned. She didn't want to complicate her life. She was honest and she liked helping people.

Donna's father was comfortable with her around the house, but he was not an easy man to be around. If he liked you, that was fine. If not, then he was difficult and didn't want you around.

Theresa never became intimate with this man. They were just friends.

The man once said to Theresa, "You are not from here, but you are very lucky that you came to Greenwich, Connecticut. You work hard and there is always money to be made here. My children embarrass me. They don't work. They are waiting for me to die. My children don't know it, but I'm leaving all of my money to strangers because they didn't follow in their mother's footsteps. When my wife was alive, she was very busy. She handled lots of different things. She gave many people jobs and she helped a lot of poor people. She donated a lot of money to India. She was a warm person. I went on many business trips to India. I saw that many of the people there had no clothes to wear and no food to eat. These children of ours have a lot of nerve. They think that their mother's money is theirs."

Theresa got to know him very well.

The man paid Theresa every week, not a large sum of money, but a normal amount. The children became even more jealous and they did not want her there. Donna called her father and told him that he better keep Theresa out of the house. She told him that she had seen Theresa with a piece of jewelry that belonged to her late mother.

Her father told her that he had bought it for his wife, but that he told Theresa that she could have it. Theresa had told him that she couldn't take it. She had only worn it a few times to let him know that she appreciated it. She was afraid of the children and she didn't want any problems, so she had given it back to him.

The man said to Theresa, "After my wife died, I should have moved out. I shouldn't have stayed here."

Before his wife died, she had let him control the company and all of its assets. He never let any of the children handle the assets because they didn't work and didn't value the company. He had controlled all the money.

"If only they would work, I would help them," he said to Theresa, "but they just hang around with no jobs."

He was the type of man who would not throw money away. He told Theresa that he went to Harvard Law School and that he had socialized with Robert and Teddy Kennedy. Sometimes they would still visit each other.

"When I was young," he said, "I met all kinds of people. I met a lot of big shots. They were very intelligent people. If I had to start all over again, it would be different. I don't know why my wife didn't teach these children to work. I couldn't control them because I am their father. They would not listen to me even if I tried. If only they had worked, knew how to pay the bills, and knew the value of the money, that's all I wanted them to know. But they never showed me that they could assume any responsibility and they didn't know what life was all about. Every time they got in trouble, their mother always bailed them out. Their mother made it all too easy for them. They all thought they were entitled to the money and they did not want to lift a finger for it. They only know the easy way. Their minds are very small."

"Look at you, Theresa, you were not born here. You work and make a decent living. I admire you. These kids always got into trouble outside and their mother always did everything for them. She thought until she died that she had taken care of the children, but she made them helpless and turned them into invalids. She really wasn't helping them at all."

"Theresa, I did a lot in my day. I worked my butt off when I was in the service. I was an officer. I was a pilot at the time of Hiroshima and I was supposed to drop a bomb on Hiroshima. I flew down toward my target and I saw a lot of women and children. I kept on going. I couldn't drop the bomb. I didn't want to be responsible for killing innocent women, children and animals. I went back and told my commander that I couldn't do it. I told him that I had seen the women, children and animals there. I told him that if he wanted to kill them, he had to send someone else. I used to throw canned food and candy from my plane. I would drop it for the women and children in the villages. I spent my whole paycheck on food for them."

He was an interesting, sensitive man. He continued to drink to control his pain. His heart was not good and he had liver problems. He always saw his lawyer two to three times per month.

Once Theresa didn't see him for a while because she was afraid of the kids. They still didn't want him to have any friends. At that time she usually came to see him twice a month. Later on Theresa came to visit him two to three times a week.

He was very sick at one time. Theresa knew an acupuncturist in New York who dealt with pain. He was supposed to go there twice a week, and the first time he went, he liked it. It reduced the pain in his back.

Instead of returning, though, he decided he wanted to stay home drinking. Theresa looked at his eyes. They were watery yellow. He had hepatitis.

It got worse, but Theresa could not go to the house for a while because the children did not want her there.

He called Theresa and asked me to come by to do some things for him. When she got there, he told her that his son had ordered him to give him a million dollars and when he refused, the son beat him with a golf club and kicked him. He said that the son must have thought he beat him to death. His body was black and blue all over.

He had to go to the hospital. Theresa went to visit him there a few times and a week later he went home.

He said to Theresa, "I was so angry with the kids. I got my lawyer to get the will set up. I left the house to Harvard along with money." He had also appointed the lawyer as executor of the will. The children could not contest the will because they couldn't afford a lawyer and because they were not competent anyway.

He had called the police. After that, the children were not allowed to come into the house any more.

His blood started clotting up, but he didn't bother to go to the doctor. He was too depressed after what the son had done to him.

He got sick again after his son had beaten him and this time he went to a New York hospital.

After that, he never recovered. Everything went wrong with him. His lawyer stayed very tight with him. Theresa did not see him at all anymore because of the children.

She couldn't even go to the funeral.

Donna had been looking for Theresa, but Theresa didn't want anything to do with the family.

All the children who had been living in Greenwich ultimately moved out of state. He did leave money to his own child, though, but his wife's children automatically went to his child then to try to get money.

CHAPTER IX
SUCCESS STRATEGIES
REGARDING EMPLOYMENT

Getting Started—Writing Your Resume

Creative job hunting begins even before a new resume is prepared.

There are several things you need to know about yourself before you start writing a resume. The first step is an in-depth self-evaluation. This includes a hard look at your experience, your temperament, and your needs and goals for obtaining employment. You want to define clearly what the perfect working situation is for you.

One way to do this is to find those things you liked about each job you have held. List out your strengths and weaknesses in each of those jobs and your major achievements in each previous job. List all your skills in order of their importance. Describe your temperament.

Now list those qualities you want in a job, for example, fast track competition or low-pressure environment, creative opportunities, etc.

If you are a professional, you can use a headhunter to help find a job.

Preparing for the Interview

Make sure when you go to an interview you go early in the morning. Never call for a job interview after ten or eleven in the morning. They'll think you can't get out of bed.

Wear subdued clothing such as navy or light colors. Your skirt should never be too short, and never wear dangling earrings or noisy jewelry to an interview.

Your hair is very important.

Don't look wild, just look attractive.

Listen to the interviewer. Never ask about money. Let him tell you.

Over-educated or Over-qualified

If you have just graduated from business school and have no experience, it can be difficult to get a job. And, just because you went to college, you might not make big money, especially right away.

You might have to take any job you can get at first just so that you can pay your bills.

If you want to apply for a job at a large company and you have just gotten out of school, you must not forget that you will need to get some experience under your belt. You will be better off taking a small job of whatever size so that you don't get depressed and upset about money.

You have to keep up with your bills. They come in every day, non-stop, and the days go by so fast. Sometimes it is hard to keep up. Even a lowly position to start will help you pay the bills.

You have to plan everything in your life together, too, so that you can have a good time and enjoy your life.

Once at work, office jealousy can be a problem. If you work hard, you can incur a lot of jealousy in the office from both men and women, but for different reasons. If you are an attractive woman, the women can be jealous or envious. You might have to downplay your looks. Don't be too showy or glamorous at work. Be low-key, but elegant and presentable. Watch what you say. Sometimes the less said, the better. Don't engage in office gossip. Rise above it. Do your work. It's important to please your boss.

Don't make too many mistakes because too many people are looking for jobs. Others at work can go after you, even those you help all the time or those you might think are your friends. They could be looking to take your job.

Don't talk to others at work about your personal life. Never. Keep your personal business to yourself. If they ask you questions, tell them nothing. Excuse yourself from the conversation or change the subject. Just say, "It's nice weather today, isn't it."

Find your friends outside of work, and if you want to talk about some personal problems or your personal life, talk only to one or two good and trusted friends. Good and trusted friends are rare and are hard to find. Remember that.

Education and Experience or Skills

What's the difference between education and experience?

The difference is that no matter how much education you have, you still need experience to be able to maneuver through life. You need to have common sense, experience and skills.

Otherwise, you can get yourself into trouble by trusting the wrong people who may be jealous of you and want to sink you because you have money and they don't. It is the syndrome of the "haves" and the "have nots." The world can be a jungle.

Act very low-key. Be humble. Don't have too many close friends, just one or two. Don't easily trust new people coming into your circle.

Be savvy. If you're dealing with a new person, you can find out about their issues by talking around the subject and yet still find out your answers.

Think five times before you open your mouth.

Speaking too fast is not good. You have to slow down because a person can create his or her own problems by talking too fast.

When you have money, the so-called friends stick to you like a magnet. But beware. When you have a problem or need help, they forget who you are. Your good friends will be there to help you, though. Even though it is a tough lesson sometimes to find out who are your true friends, it is good for you because you then will know who your real friends are and who you can count on.

Experience is valuable.

Never work as housewife. There's no experience in it. One woman, who had only worked in the home, kept applying for jobs, but no one wanted to hire her. They told her that she had no experience.

She kept looking and kept thinking that nothing was impossible, experience or no experience. She was determined. She wouldn't talk to anybody about the troubles of finding a job. She kept her problems to herself. She knew that she would find a job sooner or later.

At first she got small jobs here and there. Then she got a job and they trained her.

She held the job for a long time, and then she went to a bank to borrow money. They would not loan her money even though she had money in the bank because she had no credit. She had a trust fund, but she had lost $250,000 in the stock market crash, even after being warned it was about to come. She had not heeded good advice.

Her mind always told her that something was going to turn out well. That's a good attitude.

Attitude in life is key.

Don't forget to look at the big picture, not just at the small problems and irritations you have on a day to day basis. Make sure you can see the forest through the trees.

Some people are rich and cannot get a job because they don't have any training, any previous experience, or any job references. Always get training because you don't know when the money will run out or when something unexpected will happen, for example, a crash in the stock market, which is what happened in this woman's case.

Women Who are Over-Qualified

Some men and women are over-qualified. They don't want to take just any job because the pay is so low, but they have to keep money coming in so they don't get stuck with their bills. It's hard once you get stuck.

Even though you get paid low wages, you should keep working. Keep working while you are trying to find something else so that you don't get discouraged about finances. People are not as anxious to hire you if you are not working, either.

If you are single, you might even need two paychecks.

Hating Your Job

A person is not happy at work if there are a lot of people there who don't like him or her and try to chase the person out. They can always find reasons to chase you out. If you're over forty, it's hard to keep a job. If you seem flaky, they think you don't want to work because they think that shows in your face.

When you work in these situations, you can't concentrate because you are not happy. This is not good.

Sooner or later, you'll have to go, but some people get so confused; they don't know where to go. When you leave a company, make sure you are on good terms because you'll need a reference for the next job. Especially if you are fifty or older, it's difficult to get a good job without references from your present work.

Loving Your Job

From the first moment you get up in the morning, you can't wait to get to work when you love your job. This is positive.

When you get to the office, you say hello and you smile at everyone. You like people. You work with people. You deal with people.

If you want to get a promotion, make things happen with yourself.

Woman Working for a Company for Many Years Who Wants to Quit

Women who work for large companies must know that before they retire, the company sometimes tries to let you go or they may try to give you a part-time job. At a certain age, a company wants younger people in order to save money.

After you retire, Social Security is not a lot of money. Make sure you have saved money either in bank accounts, stocks, government bonds, real estate, even in gold bricks if you have to. You should stash away a certain percentage from every paycheck in case you lose your job. This is especially true if you are single because when it comes to money, there are very few people who will or can help you out.

CHAPTER X
OPENING YOUR OWN BUSINESS

Before she opened her store, Lori never analyzed what was actually involved in running her own business. She didn't know half the details that she was supposed to know.

Not only that, she also didn't think that she would need to spend long hours or that she would need to keep a close eye on her employees. In business, you can't close your eyes on your employees.

You can't even close your eyes on yourself.

The first thing she should have known was how much capital she needed to work with. Because she didn't know, she ran out of money before she ever started to consistently make a profit. One needs to have enough money beforehand to both set up the business and to pay its expenses for the time period it will take to consistently turn a profit, regardless if that's six months or six years.

The second thing one should focus on is the cost of rent. Some areas have very high rents, but it depends what kind of business you have if you need to pay that high an amount. If your clientele are going to expect an upscale setting, you'll have to provide it for them. Then you need to know the cost of telephone, insurance, utilities, advertising—especially the additional costs of advertising when you first open the business: that's the only way people will know you are there.

The third thing to figure out is the number of employees and how much you'll pay them weekly. And you have to pay yourself, too. In order to pay yourself, you'll need to know your expenses at home and how much money you have to have every week to live.

You have to then figure out a real expectation of the time it will take for you to make a profit. You need to factor in, too, what you have already paid for your inventory. You aren't going to make a lot of money every day to start with. If you have an expensive inventory, you may not sell a profitable item for some time after you first open up.

In other words, you have to think about and be prepared for the worst from the very start.

Don't plan on taking any vacations for a while.

Lori spent more time on vacation than she did at work. So the business went the other way from the start. She didn't really pay attention. Instead she relied on the employees to bring the business up. That was only one of her mistakes, but a big mistake.

Don't think your employees are going to work as conscientiously as you are. They're not.

Four years after Lori opened her business, she still was not making a profit. Yet she kept buying new inventory and putting it in the store. That was a mistake, too.

One day she realized she wasn't going to make it. She had far too much inventory, but no cash to pay her employees, her expenses, or herself.

She did find someone to back her so she could keep the store open, but she didn't take any inventory beforehand. She still didn't know her assets. Nor did her backer. Not only that, she still didn't know how much money to borrow. She made the same mistake she'd made when she started.

Before she had looked for a backer, she had gone to her mother. Her mother had a lot of money and "loaned" it to her. She ended up cleaning her mother out. She even got her mother to take out a second mortgage on her house.

After her mother's money was gone, and although she was lucky to find a backer to bail her out, the money never went to the right place. She spent it for decorations and to make the business a showcase rather than to pay the bills. So the money didn't actually help her and it didn't last.

The backer wasn't getting paid back. One day she went to the store, but Lori was not there. She was off on one of her vacations. The backer came back to the store and removed all her inventory.

When Lori came back, the backer accused her of taking the inventory. It was a disaster. Lori almost got locked up. There were lawyers and there were court cases, but she never got her inventory back.

She lost everything.

She didn't know what to do. Her life fell apart. She got very sick and didn't want to live anymore.

When you're in trouble, no one wants to know you.

She already had cleaned out her mother. She went to her friends to try to borrow money, but they wouldn't loan her anything. Once she had had a lot of friends, but she decided she didn't need any friends, only the customer in front of her, so she neglected those friends. She had thought that because she had a business, everything was rosy.

You should never neglect your friends because you'll never know what help you'll need some day. Sometimes your friends are even better than your family. Treat your friends well. Entertain them. If they're down, help them. Whoever has helped you, never forget them.

Lori didn't do that.

She called one friend and told her she was in trouble because of what had happened to her and to her business. She said, "I didn't do what she accused me of." She asked her friend to help her. Her friend already knew what she wanted and ended up changing her phone number so Lori couldn't call back. Lori had borrowed money from her before and never paid it back.

Never borrow money from your friends. Always borrow it from a bank. Don't loan money to your friends either. Just give it to them, if you can afford it.

All these problems came to Lori because she didn't know what to do for herself.

Here's what to do.

Take care of your self first. Don't get sick. No pills. No doctors...unless you're very, very sick. They're only a shortcut. Don't get welfare. Don't get food stamps. They're shortcuts too and they don't work.

Instead of going to your friends or trying to borrow money, fix it all yourself.

Pretend nothing has happened. Don't look for sympathy. You did this yourself. You get out of it by yourself. Life is a lot of mistakes.

Get up early in the morning. Get another job. Nobody is going to feel sorry for you because they all know you did it yourself. That's how you become strong. By fixing the mistakes in life yourself.

When you go down, it is hard to bring yourself back up. That's true. But when you have problems, you have to solve them yourself.

Take care of yourself. Get lots of exercise.

Get yourself another job. Two jobs, if you need to. Work is always good. To be with people is the most wonderful thing that can happen to you.

At work, however, when you're down and have problems, don't bother others. Everyone has work to do. Don't let others know you have problems and people will love you to death. Show people that you are strong.

Even your relationships won't work if the other thinks you have problems and even if you do talk to someone else for help, you'll still have to lift yourself up. You have to put happy thoughts in your own head, you have to get a lot of exercise, and you have to eat well. You must be by yourself for this to work.

Lori was never able to put herself together. She got sick and couldn't work because she was too wound up with all the commotion. She couldn't take it, and she ended up on welfare.

After a hardship passes, no matter what comes to you, it will be a piece of cake. We all go through this. It is not just you.

You can start all over again. But first, you have to be strong.

EPILOGUE

Once there was a woman and everything wiped her out. Her life was like a hurricane. Everything went wrong. Every time she touched things, it was as if she touched snow and it melted. She could not fix anything.

At that time, she did not have anyone. She couldn't pick herself up. This went on for a very long time. She did not want to get involved with friends because she could not talk about the calamities in her life, so she kept to herself and very quietly went about her business. She was alone. She did not talk to anybody for over ten years because she did not want to get involved with people. She just told herself, "You are going to be fine." Sometimes, she would blame herself, and she had to teach herself to stop being negative with herself.

She told herself that she got herself into this and now she had to get herself out. She knew that she had to do this for her survival. She knew that someday she was going to get the doors to open. It was as if she had been in a closet for a very long time. All she did was go to work, pick up the groceries and go home.

She did not drink, smoke or stay up late. She did not even take a vacation. She watched her diet. That was first. She ate a lot of vegetables and not too much red meat. She took her vitamins. She went to the doctor once in a while to have a check up. She would not take medication unless she was very sick. She walked a lot and she would meditate.

Sometimes she would take a ride in the country. Sometimes she would feel happy, and she would get a glass of wine and look in the mirror and give a toast, "Here's to you and me."

She would play a nice song and sing to it. Before she would go to bed, she would read the Bible. She wanted to be happy again. She just wanted to clean up the things that went wrong in her life. She had no one, so it gave her a chance to really clear her head and figure out what steps she needed to take to make things better and then go from there. She became happier because she found herself and what she wanted to do in life.

She decided to be single, just to work, and to take care of herself. This is not necessarily for everybody, but it worked for her. She did this for herself, not for anybody else.

It worked. After that, she was happy. She started to make new friends who were very nice. She started to get invited out and she met a lot of different people who were very different than she was.

From time to time, she would read their fortune. They had fun. But she never talked about her past. Mentally, she was very strong, in and out, because her father always taught her to be strong. She dreamed at night that she was flying, which carries a message with it that you are going to be healthier. It also means your life is going to be more free and independent.

And now, she is finally happy doing what she does. Her burdens have fallen by the wayside. She is happier than she has ever been in her entire life.

The woman I just described used to be me.

978-0-595-36596-8
0-595-36596-5

www.ingramcontent.com/pod-product-compliance
Lightning Source LLC
Chambersburg PA
CBHW022248290526
45785CB00015B/393